Coping with Social Anxiety

Coping with Social Anxiety

The

DEFINITIVE GUIDE *to* EFFECTIVE TREATMENT OPTIONS

Eric Hollander, M.D.,
and Nicholas Bakalar

An Owl Book

Henry Holt and Company | New York

2385336

Henry Holt and Company, LLC
Publishers since 1866
115 West 18th Street
New York, New York 10011

Henry Holt® is a registered trademark of
Henry Holt and Company, LLC.

Copyright © 2005 by Eric Hollander, M.D.,
and Nicholas Bakalar
All rights reserved.
Distributed in Canada by H. B. Fenn and Company Ltd.

Library of Congress Cataloging-in-Publication Data

Hollander, Eric, date.
   Coping with social anxiety : the definitive guide to effective treatment
options /Eric Hollander and Nicholas Bakalar.—1st ed.
            p. cm.
   Includes bibliographical references and index.
   ISBN-13: 978-0-8050-7582-3
   ISBN-10: 0-8050-7582-8
   1. Social phobia. 2. Social phobia—Treatment. I. Bakalar, Nick. II. Title.
   RC552.S62H655 2005
   616.85'225—dc22   2004059937

Henry Holt books are available for special promotions and
premiums. For details contact: Director, Special Markets.

First Edition 2005

Designed by Victoria Hartman

Printed in the United States of America
10 9 8 7 6 5 4 3 2 1

To our families

Contents

Introduction: A "New" Disease?

In the not overly polite or decorous world of the National Football League, New Orleans Saints running back Ricky Williams was known as a serious nutjob. He would sit in the locker for interviews with the press wearing his helmet—dark visor and all—answering questions in a barely audible voice. He'd stay home all day, afraid that if he went out he'd run into somebody he might have to talk to. If forced to go to a dinner, he'd hide in the men's room until the last possible moment to avoid table conversation. On the airplane, he'd sit alone, staring out the window, scrunched down in his seat. Forced to go to a supermarket to buy something, he'd run from aisle to aisle trying to avoid any contact with fans who recognized him. Billy Joe Tolliver, who was the New Orleans quarterback during Williams's rookie year, was once overheard commenting, "People in Texas call him Ricky Williams, but he's really Ricky Weirdo. I'm telling you, he's going to go postal one day." Williams spent three years with the Saints, never really living up to the high expectations the team had for this University of Texas Heisman Trophy winner.

In the 2002 season, however, Williams was traded to the Miami

Dolphins, and everything changed. The view he now usually presents to the defense is his dreadlocks flying out of the back of his helmet. They just can't catch up to him—in 2002, Williams ran for 16 touchdowns and a league-leading 1,853 yards. And it wasn't just his rushing that had improved. He had improved in more profound ways as well.

The fact is that Ricky Williams isn't a "weirdo" at all. His behavior was strange—no doubt about it—but the reason for it was that he suffered from a very common psychiatric disorder called social phobia or social anxiety. Once he learned this and sought treatment, his life began to turn around. When he first went into therapy in the spring of 2001, he felt relief that his problem had a name, and that there were others who suffered from the same disorder. As therapy continued he began to feel more comfortable with other people. Now he has stopped doing interviews with his helmet on. He's able to go to the mall and interact with the inevitable fans who approach him. He even says he has a better relationship with his daughter. As he puts it, he was "able to start acting like the real Ricky Williams."

Social anxiety—the overpowering shyness that made Williams's life miserable—is, after depression and alcoholism, the third most common psychiatric illness in the United States. It is a disease that can hit anyone—women are affected about twice as often as men, but men seek treatment more often, probably because men become more impaired in social functioning than women. And the disorder often begins in childhood. Although doctors now know how to treat it successfully, most people who suffer from it never get any treatment at all. They just suffer.

Their suffering goes far beyond the discomfort of ordinary nervousness in meeting new people or bashfulness in public situations. In fact, not all people suffering from social anxiety even consider themselves shy in the usual sense of that word, and many shy people do not meet the diagnostic criteria for social anxiety. The disorder often starts in childhood and, untreated, has lasting effects throughout life—what psychiatrists call "long-term morbidity." This long-term morbidity can affect almost everything—education, work, family, love and sex, friendship, social life—and the effects are never positive. People with social anxiety may experience persistent terror in social or performance situations that provokes relentless, crippling anxiety. The fear is so great that it interferes with their normal routines at school, work, and in social activities. They are perfectly aware that the fear is abnormal or irrational, but this knowledge doesn't help: the fear persists, uncontrollable. Attending a social gathering, giving a talk in front of a group, eating in public, even, strange as it may seem, writing in public (signing a credit card slip, for example) can create a heart-stopping terror impossible to overcome. Using a public toilet can become a physiological impossibility. In children, the fear may be manifested by crying, tantrums, shrinking from social situations, freezing when confronted with unfamiliar people. No, this is not ordinary shyness; it is a disabling illness whose cause is poorly understood. It has both psychological and physical symptoms and it can be successfully treated with proper medical and psychological attention.

Although historically well known (the term *phobie des situations sociales* was coined by a French doctor, Pierre Janet, in 1903), social anxiety was not officially recognized as a psychiatric disorder until 1980—that's when the American Psychiatric Association first included the disease in the *Diagnostic and Statistical Manual* (*DSM*), the essential reference book of psychiatry. By the mid-1980s, the disorder was being discussed in the popular press. In December 1984, the *New York Times* published an article entitled "Social Anxiety: New Focus Leads to Insights and Therapy." The article outlined the situations in which social anxiety disorder is likely to occur—parties with strangers, giving a speech, being asked personal questions in public, meeting a date's parents, and so on. Then it discussed therapies, emphasizing that therapy for this disorder doesn't usually concentrate on deep hidden causes or the patient's childhood conflicts, but rather on practical and straightforward techniques for eliminating fear. The kinds of therapy described were similar to the cognitive therapies that will be discussed later in this book. The author of the article mentioned briefly that there was some research that appeared to demonstrate that social anxiety had a physiological component—that it was in some sense "built in" in certain children, and that the trait tended to persist as the child aged. The article put the number of people suffering from the clinical extreme of social anxiety at about 2 percent of the population.

Fifteen years later, in May 1999, the *Times* published another article on social anxiety. The title this time was "A Bold Rush to Sell Drugs to the Shy: Huge Market Expected to Treat Social Phobia." It begins not with a discussion of how many people consider themselves shy, as the 1984 article did, but rather with personal testimony from a college freshman who "suffers from an extreme form of shyness called social phobia." He has never dated, never goes to bars or restaurants or ball games. His chest tightens every time he is around people. "I am not a loner by choice," he says. "I like being with people, but I always get scared and nervous." Social anxiety itself is described differently from the way it was described in the earlier article: it is the third most common psychiatric illness, affecting nearly 19 million Americans—not the 2 percent of the population mentioned in 1984, but as much as 9 percent. Many of them are so shy they can't even make an appointment to see a therapist, "but," the author writes rather glibly, "it does not require group therapy to pop a pill." Then the article gets to the point: Prozac, Zoloft, Effexor, and Luvox, medicines used to treat depression, are now being tested and found effective in treating social anxiety as well, and drug companies are eager to begin marketing them for this purpose. Having made the motives of the drug companies perfectly clear, the author evenhandedly demonstrates the self-interest of those insisting that drugs are not the answer—the psychologists, social workers, and other therapists running "institutes" where expensive psychological tests are undertaken, time-consuming therapies are carried out, and tapes and books are sold. Each therapy, it is clear, has its strengths and weaknesses, opinions vary even among experts, and self-interested parties, the article emphasizes, are everywhere.

***

Is social anxiety not really a disease at all, but just an invention of people who want to make money by selling drugs and other therapies to treat it? Is this another symptom of the "medicalization" of human behavior? Can't a person overcome shyness by an act of will? Why can't she just face facts, pull herself together, stop acting like a frightened child? Why can't she just grow up? Even though they can be asked crudely, these are difficult questions that raise complex issues of free will and are matters of profound belief, of politics, philosophy, and even religion. You will not learn any definitive answers to such questions in this book—I'm not a philosopher, only a doctor—but I have to make my own position clear at the outset.

All human disease, medical and psychiatric, is a human invention. There are no diseases out there in nature—just natural phenomena. When these natural phenomena affect us in negative ways, we call them diseases. This is as true of infectious disease as it is of any psychiatric disorder. A flu virus is not a "disease." It's not even a disease if it gets inside you. It's not a disease, in fact, until it causes symptoms and gives you the flu. Similarly, "feeling sad" is not a disease until the sadness becomes an overpowering interference with normal life. When it does, we call it "clinical depression" (among other terms) and we treat it as the disease it is. So it is with shyness. No, being shy is not a disease or a disorder. But when shyness begins to interfere with work and school, love and sex, successful close relationships, and more, then we classify it as a psychiatric disorder, and we treat it.

Psychiatric illnesses—diseases of the brain—are sometimes more difficult for people to accept as "real" than other diseases. Few would question the reality of a psychiatric disease like schizophrenia, whose symptoms, which include delusions and hallucinations, are so vivid and obvious that clearly something has upset the normal functioning of a bodily organ, the brain. Some still question the reality of clinical depression, though fewer and fewer do as we learn more about brain function and as treatment for depression becomes more and more effective. Probably more people question the reality of a brain disorder called social anxiety—although those who suffer from it are in general not among them. If you are still in doubt about the reality of social anxiety as a disease, you may find the concluding chapter of this book persuasive. Here we discuss some of the research that is beginning to locate social anxiety in specific brain pathways that control social behavior. So for many reasons, which will become clear as you read this book, social anxiety is a brain disorder that can be successfully treated.

Failing to treat social anxiety disorder has serious consequences, both for the individual and for society in general. People with social anxiety have high rates of outpatient medical treatment and high rates of suicide. They are more likely to be financially dependent and to suffer from other psychiatric illnesses, particularly alcohol abuse. Their functioning at work and in school is more likely to be impaired, and the general state of their health is poorer than the rest of the population. Yet despite these data, established in careful studies, many people still consider social anxiety disorder a trivial complaint, unworthy of serious medical attention.

In a large midwestern health maintenance organization, the Dean Health Plan, those with social anxiety were 10 percent less likely to graduate from college, earned 10 percent less than those without the disorder, and were about 14 percent less likely to be in a technical, managerial, or professional position. People with social anxiety disorder had significantly greater overall work impairment and missed a greater percentage of work time than those without the diagnosis. They had thoughts of suicide more than six times as often as those without the diagnosis—in fact, lifetime suicide attempt rates were as high in people with social anxiety disorder as in those with major depression. They even cost the HMO more money per year— $2,536 for those with a diagnosis of social anxiety versus $1,887 for those with no psychiatric diagnosis. It is possible that early and aggressive treatment of social anxiety disorder may have saved the HMO some money by eliminating its expensive-to-treat problems that often accompany it, yet the disorder was largely undiagnosed or undertreated. To me, this doesn't make a lot of sense.

⚬

The terms "social phobia" and "social anxiety" are used interchangeably in the research in this field. I will use both terms, and I'll sometimes use the abbreviation SAD (not to be confused with seasonal affective disorder, which is entirely different). Calling the illness "social phobia" rather than "social anxiety disorder," some experts feel, implies that it is similar to a phobia about snakes or heights, which it is not. It is a pervasive disorder, affecting many aspects of the sufferer's life. These mental health professionals believe that calling it a phobia may in some cases minimize its seriousness, discourage primary care physicians from diagnosing it as a psychiatric disorder distinct from others, and result in a failure to treat it properly. Patients who suffer from social anxiety rarely bring it to the attention of their doctors—the doctors have to ask about it. And unless doctors consider it a distinct and serious illness, they won't ask. Still, many psychiatrists and psychiatric researchers still use the term social phobia, and in fact, this is the term used in the *Diagnostic and Statistical Manual.* When you see the term social phobia in this book, it should be taken as a synonym for social anxiety disorder.

Our understanding of social anxiety and its treatment has changed radically over the past two decades. We are now aware that the disorder is not rare, but actually one of the more common psychiatric illnesses. Psychological therapies have been better tested, new drugs have been developed, and there is more scientific research being undertaken on social anxiety than ever before. But the scientific data are complex and difficult to understand, the medicines we use vary widely in their efficacy and have many undesirable side effects, and there is still plenty of controversy about psychological versus medical treatments. It's enough to make the average person's head spin. This book is an attempt to clarify and explain these developments, and to give guidance to those seeking to overcome a confusing, troubling, and sometimes devastating disorder.

Coping with Social Anxiety

Part One

Who Gets Social Anxiety, and Why?

Some human characteristics are purely genetic. Eye color is one of them. No amount of "good" or "bad" parenting, no physical environment, north or south, hot or cold, will change the color of a baby's eyes. Others—the language we speak, for example—are purely environmental. There are no genes for speaking English, or French, or Navajo. But most human qualities, particularly those that have to do with behavioral and emotional traits, seem to lie somewhere in the messy middle—a complex combination of genetic and environmental factors that work together to make us what we are. It is often extremely difficult to say exactly what environment or genes contributes to a given characteristic, and so it is with social anxiety disorder (SAD). Much scientific effort has gone into trying to figure out how much the symptoms of social anxiety disorder can be attributed to our genes and how much can be attributed to our environment. While little is known definitively, researchers have developed considerable data that suggest at least some partial answers to this difficult question.

Childhood Trauma and Social Anxiety

Current estimates are that somewhere between 4 and 8 percent of adults suffer from SAD in any year, and that the percentage of people suffering from the disorder at some time in their lives is even higher. Such a rate makes social anxiety, after depression and alcoholism, the third most common psychiatric disorder. Knowing how many people suffer from a disease is, of course, not enough. We'd like to be able to predict which people are going to suffer from a given disease so that we can intervene early to prevent it. To do this, researchers look for risk factors—clues that suggest a disease is likely to occur. In the case of social anxiety (and many other psychiatric illnesses) one of the things they look for is developmental problems in childhood. If a particular kind of childhood problem leads to later social anxiety disorder, it is identified as a risk factor for the disorder, one of the contributing causes of a disease. This is what a team of Canadian researchers did in 2001 when they set about to examine the backgrounds of people with SAD. They depended for their data on a large health survey undertaken by the Ontario Ministry of Health.

The study found that certain childhood events are highly correlated with SAD later in life. Childhood sexual abuse, the lack of a close relationship with an adult, failure in early grades of school, and dropping out of high school were all associated with SAD. So were moving more than three times as a child, involvement with the juvenile justice system, and running away from home. Social class, on the other hand, had no bearing whatsoever on whether a person would suffer from the disorder. Being a firstborn male increased the risk for social anxiety; firstborn females experienced no such increased risk.

But things are never so simple. The authors of the study are careful to point out that these associations are not the same as causes. It is perfectly plausible, for example, that a child who runs away from home is already suffering from a form of social anxiety, so that it isn't running away that caused social anxiety, but the social anxiety that caused the running away. The same problem might apply to any other of the risk factors identified. So the authors' correlations, accurate though they are, tell little about whether these childhood events actually cause social anxiety.

Childhood trauma seems to play a role in other closely related anxiety diseases as well. Panic disorder and generalized anxiety disorder have both been found to be significantly related to past childhood physical or sexual abuse—in fact, in some studies these disorders appear to be more closely related to such abuse than social anxiety disorder.

Childhood behavior, even when it isn't pathological, might also be a predictor of social anxiety disorder. I see some kids who seem naturally curious; they like to explore new environments, meet new people. Others are more withdrawn. Inhibited behavior—a consistent tendency in children to display fear and withdrawal in any new situation—gives me a hint that social anxiety will develop. A carefully designed study published in 2001 demonstrated that behavioral inhibition was associated with a higher risk for SAD as well as other anxiety disorders. (There was also some good news for shy kids: behavioral inhibition has a lower association with disruptive behavior.)

The next question is why childhood personality or behavior predicts social anxiety in adulthood, and the answer is not at all self-evident. Many feel that childhood experience makes people modify their attitudes about the world and the extent to which they fear it. Some speculate that childhood trauma actually causes biological changes in the brain that lead to social anxiety, and this finds some support in animal studies. By manipulating the environment of young macaque monkeys, and then testing their reactions to anxiety-provoking drugs later in life, researchers were able to show that a stressful environment in juveniles was likely to produce anxious adults, and even actual permanent neuronal changes in the animals' brains caused by early experience.

The experiment worked like this. Two groups of five female macaques and their infants were the subjects. In the first group, mothers had easy access to their food rations. In the second group, mothers had to search for their food in a device that hid the rations under a pile of wood chips. This required considerable time—and considerable anxiety—in finding the food. Both groups of infants matured normally, but the second group were raised by anxious parents. Presumably this anxiety would affect their treatment of their infants.

When the infants were six months old, the researchers gave them anti-anxiety drugs. The infants raised by anxious mothers responded more to the drugs as measured by observations of their social behavior than did those raised by non-anxious parents. Apparently, anxious mothers had transmitted their anxiety to their children, even to the extent of causing biological changes that would result in a different response to anti-anxiety medicines.

But of course I treat people, not monkeys, and it has been almost impossible for researchers to connect a specific traumatic event in a person's life to the development of social anxiety disorder. A minority of patients report a specific event that they feel led to the development of their problem, but their reports are not always reliable. Often there is a long delay between the time a patient feels symptoms and the time he seeks help, and in the interval many traumatic events may have happened and been forgotten. It is probably true that traumatic events by themselves are unlikely to be the cause of social anxiety—significant proportions of people without social anxiety have experienced traumatic events, and some studies show as little as 15 percent of those with social anxiety can point to a specific traumatic event as the source of their problem.

Nevertheless, there are some suggestive findings about less dramatic or specific events. Constant rejection or bullying by peers, for example, may sensitize kids who are already at risk for social anxiety. One study found that "behavioral inhibition" in five- to twelve-year-olds (assessed by parents looking back at the past), long-lasting separation from parents, and a parental history of psychopathology were all associated with the incidence of social anxiety. Whether or not any of these things are actual causes of social anxiety, however, is another unanswered question.

Genes and Your Destiny

If it is differences in brain structure that cause a tendency to social anxiety, then it is clear that genetics may also play a part. Everyone notices that "the apple doesn't fall far from the tree," that not only physical appearance but also children's behavior tends to resemble that of their parents. But noticing such similarities is not the same as scientifically proving that they are inherited, and certainly far from proving exactly what the mechanism of inheritance is. The inheritance of physical traits—eye and hair color, height, weight, and so on—is complicated enough. When it comes to the inheritance of behavioral traits, the complexity increases enormously, and the uncertainties begin to multiply.

That shyness is inherited is not a new observation. In 1872, Charles Darwin published *The Expression of Emotion in Man and Animals,* in which he asserted that shyness—or at least its physiological manifestation in blushing—was an inherited characteristic. He quotes the observations of a physician: "Even peculiarities in blushing seem to be inherited. Sir James Paget, whilst examining the spine of a girl, was struck at her singular manner of blushing; a big splash of red appeared first on one cheek, and then other splashes, variously scattered over the face and neck. He subsequently asked the mother whether her daughter always blushed in this peculiar manner; and was answered, 'Yes, she takes after me.' Sir J. Paget then perceived that by asking this question he had caused the mother to blush; and she exhibited the same peculiarity as her daughter." In 1890, William James, in *The Principles of Psychology*, quoting Darwin approvingly, counted shyness as a basic human instinct.

SAD clearly runs in families. But to say that something "runs in the family" is not the same as saying it is carried in the genes. Sorting out what is genetic and what is environmental is the most difficult part of the problem. One way to do this is with twin studies. Since identical twins have exactly the same genes, differences in twins' behavior can, at least with greater justification than those between non-twins, be attributed to their environment. Most researchers agree that environment adds to whatever effect genes have—in other words, that the effect of genes is consistent no matter what the environment. If this is so, then the special case of identical twins who have been separated at birth and raised in different environments provides the ideal natural experiment to test such ideas: the genes are the same, only the environment is different. Such groups of identical twins have been studied to test all sorts of hypotheses about nature and nurture, among them the heritability of anxiety disorders.

Of course, even such an apparently perfect natural experiment has its complications and limitations. Events in a family may profoundly affect one twin while leaving the other untouched. Suppose, to take an extreme example, one twin is sexually abused by a parent while the other is not. Such an event could cause a predisposition to later psychiatric illness in the affected twin, but not in the other. Or suppose, less spectacularly, that each twin simply reacts in a different way to an event they both experience, one interpreting it as benign, the other as traumatic. Parents' frequent loud arguments with each other, for example, could be harmful or not, depending on each twin's interpretation of the meaning of these disputes.

Even twin studies sometimes contradict each other. For example, a 1992 study of 2,163 female twins concluded that 30 to 40 percent of the development of social phobia is genetically passed from parent to child. But then another study appeared to show that genetic contribution was minimal, and though some anxiety disorders seemed to be heritable, there was no difference in heritability of social anxiety between monozygotic (identical) and dizygotic (fraternal) twins. In other words, though there is some genetic component, it does not seem to be particularly strong.

More recent twin studies, conducted with more sophisticated methodologies, have shown a higher heritability of social anxiety. And they have shown that the most severe kinds of social anxiety are the most likely to run in families. Moreover, social anxiety was found to be more heritable than other kinds of anxiety disorders.

In addition to twin studies, there are studies that consider the families of people with social anxiety. It's pretty clear that having one parent with an anxiety disorder increases a child's risk of social anxiety, and that having two parents with an anxiety disorder increases it even further.

The handful of studies that specifically consider the heritability of social anxiety disorder (separate from other anxiety disorders) show that a person with a first-degree relative (a brother, sister, mother, or father) who has social anxiety is two to three times as likely to suffer from it as someone who has no such relative, and the heritability is greater for generalized social anxiety (the fear of most social situations) than for the specific form (the fear of only one or two social situations).

Parents and kids interact, whatever their genetic makeup, and different kids interact in different ways with the same parents. It's possible, for example, that a very shy and retiring child may inspire different behavior from his parents than his outgoing and sociable sibling. In such a case, parents and children work together to create two different environments for two different kinds of children. This, too, might be considered an effect of genes—the same genes that make a child shy also have an influence on his environment, in the sense that his shyness makes people interact with him in particular ways. Genetic predisposition affects environment; environment affects the expression of a genetic predisposition. One study made this stunningly clear, when researchers looked at adoptive parents of children whose biological parents suffered from substance abuse or antisocial personality. The researchers first showed that the bad behavior of the children was significantly related to the psychiatric diagnosis of their biological parents. This was interesting, but not surprising. But then they showed that children who behaved badly (presumably genetically induced behavior, since they had no contact with their biological parents) elicited less nurturance and more hostility from their adoptive parents. Thus the behavior of the adoptive parents was significantly influenced by the psychiatric status of the biological parents, even though they had never come into contact with each other! The biological parents' genes, in other words, had, insofar as their children inherited those genes, affected the behavior of the adoptive parents. The researchers were able to draw a direct line between the psychiatric status of the biological parents and the behavior of the adoptive parents. Sorting out nature and nurture, genes and environment can be a tortuous process.

Good Parents and Bad

How about poor parenting? Can that cause psychiatric illness? Maybe, but it's not easy to decide whether someone has had poor parenting. First, how do you define "poor parenting"? Why do the same parents have such apparently varying effects on siblings? How does a child's perceptions of his parents, accurate or not, affect psychopathology? Do parents engage in different kinds of child-rearing practices depending on the personality of the child? How much of parenting style depends on the relationship between a particular child and the parents? How do you separate all the other influences, environmental and genetic, from the "parenting" factor? And, as I suggested above in discussing how children and parents interact, the behavior of the kids themselves can under some circumstances make parents "good" or "bad." Such complications make it very difficult to pin it on the parents, and when studies are undertaken that try to take all these problems into account, researchers, even those using carefully designed twin studies, can't definitively say that people's psychiatric distress is caused by having had unskilled parents.

This doesn't mean that parents have no influence, however. It seems to be true that people who suffer from social anxiety have children who are more likely to suffer from it, too. In a study published in 2000, researchers concluded that social anxiety in parents is definitely a risk factor for social anxiety in their children. The authors didn't draw any conclusions about whether this association was due to genetics or environment—they only asserted that it exists. They speculate, however, that if there are environmental factors involved, they might include a restricted opportunity to learn social skills among children of parents who don't demonstrate such skills themselves and can't teach them to their kids. Depression, alcohol use disorders, and other anxiety disorders in parents were also associated with the development of social anxiety in their offspring, although the authors admit that other studies seem to contradict this finding.

When the researchers eliminated from consideration the parents' psychiatric illnesses, they were left with one consistent factor: parental style as perceived by the child with social anxiety. Adolescents who felt their parents were either overprotective or very rejecting were more likely to have social anxiety than other kids.

You may be thinking, Well, so what? All kids have criticisms of their parents, and anyway, their recollections of the way their parents behaved often aren't that accurate. That's true, but other studies don't depend on kids' recollections of their parents' attitudes but on objective assessments of shy and non-shy mothers and children. One British study demonstrated that the mothers of shy children had considerably higher rates of anxiety disorders, especially social anxiety, than did the mothers of non-shy children. Again, the researchers didn't draw any conclusions about genetics or environment—they just stated what they found to be the case: that shy children are about seven times as likely as non-shy children to have mothers who suffer from social anxiety.

We'll have more to say about parenting in chapter 6, but I have to emphasize that I'm not an expert in parenting—nothing in my training in medical school or internship or residency qualifies me to be handing out advice about raising kids. I have kids of my own, and I think I've raised them well, but I'm not in the advice-dispensing business, especially in something as fraught with problems as bringing up children. With those warnings in mind, however, let me say this: parents who recognize themselves in the descriptions above may want to think about their own issues and how they might affect the behavior of their children. As you'll learn in reading this book, there is plenty that parents can do without running themselves down, feeling guilty, or blaming themselves for their kids' problems.

Men and Women

What part does gender play in social anxiety? Are women more susceptible than men? Probably not—the disorder affects women and men in roughly equal numbers. In general, women seek treatment for psychiatric disorders more frequently than men, but this isn't the case for social anxiety disorder. A greater percentage of men seek treatment for social anxiety than for any other anxiety disorder, and most treatment programs reflect the epidemiology of the disease in the community—about half the patients are men. There are probably several reasons for this.

Shyness, acceptable and sometimes perhaps even encouraged in women, is incompatible with traditional male sex roles and very much discouraged in men. Men are expected to be dominant and self-confident, not reticent and retiring. Parents, especially fathers, often agree with this tradition, seeing shyness in their sons as much more of a problem than the same trait in their daughters. It may also be that being shy is more disruptive to the life of a man than of a woman, and that this is another reason why men are eager to seek help with the problem. Men are supposed to initiate sexual relationships, be ambitious in their careers, speak and act boldly. Those who don't, or can't, are likely to see this as a significant life problem. There is some justification for this point of view; for example, shy men marry, become parents, and enter a stable career later in life than their more outgoing peers.

Women, too, experience problems in their professional lives if they are extremely shy. They are, for example, less likely to continue working after marriage or return to work after childbirth than non-shy women. In certain specific situations, differences between men and women are sharper: men experience more severe fear in urinating in a public restroom than women; men find returning goods to a store harder than women do; women are more likely than men to fear speaking in public, being observed while working, talking to an authority, and being the center of attention. In anxiety provoked by social situations, such as going to a party, men and women are about equally matched. They're also equally matched in the anxiety provoked by many other kinds of situations: participating in small groups, drinking or eating in public places, meeting strangers, telephoning in public, resisting a high-pressure salesman, and taking a test, among others.

In general, men and women differ more in the degree of fear they feel than in the situations that make them fearful. Especially in work situations, women report greater levels of anxiety than men. In one study, where the average age of people with social phobia was thirty-five, half of the patients were unmarried. You might guess that since it is men who are usually the ones expected to be more assertive in romantic relationships that there would be fewer unmarried men than unmarried women in such a sample—but you would be wrong. Men and women were unmarried in equal numbers.

Social anxiety in men and women is accompanied at about the same rate by diagnoses of other mood and anxiety disorders despite the fact that such disorders are usually more prevalent among women. (I'll have more to say about this in chapter 4.)

Boys and Girls

If asked, most people would agree that girls are, in general, shyer than boys, and therefore they might guess that girls are more likely to suffer from social anxiety. I certainly have this feeling. But it's difficult to establish this common observation as a scientific fact. Using questionnaires, interviews, and reports from parents, some researchers tried to figure out if there were any differences among preadolescents. They didn't have much luck finding any—boys and girls seemed quite similar in this respect. Reading aloud in front of the class, performing musically or athletically, joining in on a conversation, speaking to adults, starting a conversation, and writing on the blackboard troubled boys and girls alike. They did note, however, that parents usually thought of their daughters as significantly more anxious than their sons, even though the kids rated themselves equally fearful. This may mean that girls express their anxiety more freely than boys, but it's difficult to say. (More about this in chapter 6.) The researchers looked at race as well, and found no significant difference between whites and African-Americans.

I see a lot of kids with social anxiety, and the picture they present is disturbing. They suffer substantial emotional distress and are significantly impaired in the ways they function with their families and peers. They are lonely and largely friendless, and they resist any involvement in extracurricular activities. Their anxiety has what psychiatrists call "somatic" aspects—that is, they suffer physical symptoms like headaches and stomachaches with greater frequency than their less anxious peers. And there is another sad aspect to their plight: because they are quiet and not disruptive, they don't attract the attention that kids get when they suffer from more obtrusive behavioral problems. They cause no trouble, except to themselves. They suffer in silence.

Culture and Illness

Social anxiety disorder exists not only in Western cultures but in others as well. In Japanese and other Eastern cultures, for example, a disorder called *taijin kyofusho* is characterized by a fear of offending other people, which leads to pathological social avoidance. While this may not be exactly the same disorder as SAD, its symptoms overlap considerably with it, and it apparently responds to the same kinds of pharmacological treatments. Some believe that the underlying psychobiological mechanisms are the same in each disorder, and that culture determines the expression of the problem. People who suffer from *taijin kyofusho* typically worry about having an unpleasant body odor, stuttering, and blushing, and these concerns lead to a fear of and withdrawal from social interactions. Some have theorized that those who suffer from *taijin kyofusho* are more afraid of offending others than they are of embarrassing themselves, while social anxiety disorder sufferers in the West typically consider embarrassing themselves the bigger threat.

How Many People Have Social Anxiety Disorder?

Several epidemiological studies have now been undertaken to try to establish the prevalence of SAD in the American population. There have been two large population-based studies of the prevalence of SAD, the Epidemiological Catchment Area (ECA) and the National Comorbidity Survey (NCS). These are both large multisite studies of the prevalence and incidence of psychiatric disorders in the United States. Results from the ECA showed a lifetime prevalence among women of 3.1 percent and among men of 2.0 percent. Some sites reported higher lifetime prevalence rates for the general population— the Duke University site, for example, found a rate of 3.8 percent. A 1992 European study found an almost identical prevalence rate. But then the first study using a structured diagnostic interview was carried out by the NCS in 1998. Using these more accurate diagnostic procedures, the results were radically different: the lifetime prevalence among women was 15.5 percent, and among men 11.1 percent. With this refined diagnostic technique, we get a more accurate picture of the prevalence of the disease.

All of the studies except this last one had used the definition of social anxiety from the *Diagnostic and Statistical Manual*'s third edition. When the fourth edition, the *DSM-IV*, was published, it presented somewhat stricter criteria for making the diagnosis (see page 37). Using these criteria, a German study in 1998 concluded that SAD prevalence rates were 9.5 percent for females and 4.9 percent for males, an overall rate of 7.3 percent. In any case, most studies agree that even those individuals whose SAD is mild—that is, they meet only some of the criteria for diagnosing the disorder—could still benefit from treatment. No matter how you figure it, this is a large number of sufferers.

The Origins of Social Anxiety

Why does such irrational behavior as that associated with social anxiety arise in the first place? There are, loosely speaking, three different theories: neurobiological or evolutionary, behavioral, and cognitive. No strong argument supports one theory over the other two, and each has its logic, its supporting scientific evidence, and its proponents.

An evolutionary advantage may be conferred by a well-developed sense of fear that results in the life-preserving fight-or-flight reaction in the part of the nervous system not under conscious control, the sympathetic nervous system. Our ancestors who quickly reacted by running away from dangerous animals, for example, were the ones who survived to reproduce. Whatever genetic physiological mechanisms allowed them to do that survive in their offspring. In fact, psychophysiological research shows the similarity of this fight-or-flight reaction to that of people who are phobic about animals. In other words, those with animal phobias presumably react the same way as our predator-fearing ancestors. Since the young are most vulnerable to predators, these kinds of fears should arise very early in development, yet such is not the case with social anxiety, which arises in early adolescence or early adulthood after a person has had experience with social interactions. Proponents of an evolutionary theory respond to this objection by arguing that social fears might well have evolved as a response to the building of social hierarchies: those humans who properly understand their place in a social organization are more likely to survive and reproduce, so high anxiety about social relationships is an important survival mechanism.

Behaviorists see the development of social anxiety as an unconscious result of trauma: a child bitten by a dog develops a fear of dogs that is then irrationally applied to all dogs, whether they are a danger or not. Analogously, social anxiety results from a traumatic social experience, being humiliated, or being the object of anger or criticism on a specific occasion, which develops into an irrational fear of many or all social interactions. It is true that a large percentage of people suffering from SAD report a specific traumatic "conditioning experience." Often my patients will tell me of a specific event or events from long ago that they're sure is the root cause of their anxiety. There is at least some anecdotal evidence that witnessing another person being criticized or humiliated in a social situation might be a traumatic experience that could help cause social anxiety, and experiments with rhesus monkeys provide experimental evidence as well. The question of whether such trauma is a cause or an effect of social anxiety disorder in humans, however, remains unanswered.

There is also a cognitive model of the origins of social anxiety. Because some people lack social skills, the theory goes, they find little success in social situations. This causes them to expect bad outcomes, leading to negative thoughts about any future social interactions. These negative thoughts then cause psychological and physiological reactions that encourage avoidance of social interaction. Avoidance of social interaction limits the opportunity to practice social skills, the lack of practice perpetuates and reinforces the lack of skills, and the cycle continues. In this formulation, a person could enter the vicious cycle at any point and find himself spiraling toward social anxiety.

❧

Whatever theory they offer for its origins, and whatever the epidemiological studies demonstrate about its extent, all researchers agree that social anxiety is a common disorder, and one that disrupts lives in serious ways. You, and those you love, are not alone, and we've learned many ways to help, both medical and psychological. Picking up this book is a good beginning.

Shyness, Phobia, Social Anxiety

When people learn that I work with patients with social anxiety, they sometimes ask me whether I really believe that social anxiety disorder is a real disease. After all, lots of people are shy, and almost everyone is shy some of the time. Why would I imagine that this requires the attention of a doctor? The question is legitimate, but its answer is more complex and nuanced than some of the people who ask it may realize.

Of course, "being shy" is not an illness. It doesn't require professional care, and neither I nor any other psychiatrist I know would advise you to take medicine or undergo expensive and time-consuming psychological treatment if your only complaint is that you sometimes feel a bit reticent. There is no psychiatric diagnosis called "feeling a bit bashful sometimes," and no recognized treatment for it, and if you view being bashful sometimes as a problem, a mental health professional would probably be of no more (or less) help than anyone else in finding a solution for you.

Almost everyone at one time or another experiences some degree of some kind of anxiety. Anxiety often serves a useful, even lifesaving, purpose; for example, if an unknown person presents a threat to health or life, one's hesitation at interacting with him could be a useful survival tactic. As such, anxiety is normal, and this may be one reason why people, including many doctors, don't see social anxiety, even in its most severe and debilitating forms, as a disorder. Apprehension about interacting with other people? That's not a disease. That's life! But the failure to distinguish a temporary feeling of anxiety from the overwhelmingly destructive symptoms of social anxiety can be catastrophic. So let's get some definitions straight.

Defining Social Anxiety

The latest revision of *The Diagnostic and Statistical Manual IV–Text Revision (DSM-IV-TR)* outlines the specific criteria for arriving at a diagnosis of social anxiety. "Feeling a bit bashful sometimes," needless to say, is not among them. To be diagnosed with social phobia (as the *DSM-IV-TR* still calls it, despite the now generally preferred term social anxiety) a person has to have a persistent and distinct belief that he or she will be severely embarrassed and humiliated if put under the scrutiny of other people. The fear of social situations must provoke anxiety to the extent of having a panic attack—that is, a physiological reaction to the situation such as increased heartbeat, tremors, sweating, or nausea. Contemplation of facing a social situation has to interfere significantly with the person's normal functioning in school, at work, or in interpersonal relationships. It is a pervasive fear, and not a response to a single especially troubling public event. Most significantly, the person has to recognize that the fear is excessive, unreasonable, and unrealistic. When a patient I interview meets all these criteria (and a few others), I know that she's not just "bashful." She's suffering from a psychiatric illness called social anxiety, and there are effective treatments I can offer her.

❖ COLLEGE DAYS

I had a patient named Stephanie, a twenty-year-old college student who came into my office and told me she had always been shy in social situations, but she now felt that this shyness was really holding her back. She was an attractive young woman, articulate and intelligent, well groomed, with long dark hair and stylish clothes—not the kind of person who at first glance you would imagine could be suffering. At the same time, she was quiet and reserved, hesitant in her speech, and tense in her facial expression. She seemed to have difficulty making eye contact with me, and I often had to encourage her to speak louder. She desperately wanted to have friends, but her social interactions were so marked by feelings of being scrutinized, judged, and humiliated that she was finding it impossible to carry through with ordinary kinds of social discourse.

Stephanie said that she had been shy from early in childhood, and that though she wanted to interact with others, to make friends, she had always found it painful. She was fearful of not being accepted, not being good enough. Her parents encouraged her to engage socially, but her reluctance to do so left her feeling lonely, excluded from most activities and friendly with no one her own age. Her shyness affected her school work as well. Even though she was quite bright and easily followed what was going on in class, it was hard for her to participate. Making a presentation in class was extremely difficult. She'd suffer from upset stomachs for days before, or sometimes feign illness to get out of going to school that day. Yet she was an excellent student who had been accepted by a good four-year liberal arts college in another state. She was determined to go there and had her parents put down a deposit on the tuition and dorm room, but much as she wanted to, she couldn't follow through. Instead, she elected to attend a community college in her hometown so that she could avoid having to face the social pressures of living with other kids in a completely new environment. Predictably, living at home made everything worse. Since she didn't live on campus, she found it harder to be included in school activities, and living at home kept her more isolated than ever. This was a girl who was not just shy, but was really suffering—it was obvious to her that she had a severe problem, and after a few minutes of speaking with her, it became obvious to me as well.

The definition and diagnosis of social anxiety has evolved with new research over the decades since it was first recognized as a psychiatric disorder in 1980. At its first mention in the *DSM III,* social phobia was thought of as a fear specifically of public performance and was distinguished from "avoidant personality disorder," which was viewed as a much more generalized fear of all or most public situations. This had consequences for treatment: people with personality disorders are not generally treated with medications; those with social anxiety are. So this left many people without treatment who almost certainly could have benefited from it. By 1987, when the *DSM-III-R* was published, a subtype of social phobia had been added to include those who feared "most" social situations, not just performances. This development has created its own problems. There was no category for those who fear multiple, but not most social situations; the exact meaning of the word *most* wasn't clear, and distinguishing social anxiety from avoidant personality disorder was still almost impossible. Although the latest *DSM* edition, the *DSM-IV-TR,* still defines social phobia in much the same way, it also urges professionals to consider the diagnosis of avoidant personality disorder as comorbid, that is, existing simultaneously with social phobia. Most important, the new definition now includes children, and this has opened new areas of research and led to new ideas about the evolution of the disorder.

None of this means that deciding who has or doesn't have social anxiety disorder is always clear and straightforward. The symptoms vary across a wide spectrum, and the subjective feelings of the patient (and usually some nonspecific physical symptoms) are the only evidence for the illness—there's no lab test for it. And, of course, just about everyone experiences anxiety at one time or another. So there is always a degree of judgment involved in arriving at the diagnosis even when that judgment is well grounded in knowledge and experience.

Specific Phobia

If a person fears open spaces but no other situation in which he can be observed by others, then he probably doesn't have social anxiety but rather a specific phobia. Specific phobias are quite common, and they usually are provoked by something that causes distress at some level in the general population—fear of snakes, heights, or deep water, for example, are common. Probably a majority of people are at least a little bit afraid of such things at some time or another, and those who want to can usually avoid them. But people with specific phobias greatly overestimate the seriousness of the danger involved in such things, and their fear can be provoked even by the anticipation of confronting the feared phenomenon or object. Their fear almost always results in a panic attack with physiological symptoms, and it is severe enough to interfere with the person's normal pursuits. People suffering from phobias know that the fear is irrational, but that knowledge doesn't help them control the terror.

Experimental evidence actually shows that social anxiety is a disorder different from specific phobia and different from other anxiety disorders. Researchers selected a group of people who met the criteria for social phobia but no other anxiety disorder and a group who had no psychiatric diagnosis. Then they interviewed their families. They found three times the rate of social phobia among the first-degree relatives (that is, mothers, fathers, brothers, and sisters) of people who had social phobia as among the relatives of those who had no psychiatric diagnosis. And—this may be the most significant fact—they found that the relatives of people with social phobia had an increased risk for social phobia, but not an increased risk for any other anxiety disorder. In other words, social phobia appears to be much more heritable than other anxiety disorders, which is further evidence that it is a separate and distinct illness.

You have probably seen those long lists of Greek-derived words for specific phobias (ailurophobia = fear of cats; agoraphobia = fear of open spaces; etc.), but psychiatrists usually don't classify phobias this way. Instead, they group them into specific types of phobia: animal type, natural environment type (heights, storms, floods), blood injection–injury type, situational type (closed spaces, airplanes), and a catchall called "other type" that includes fears of choking, vomiting, and contracting an illness, among others.

Specific phobias exist independent of any other kind of behavior, and sometimes a person who seems quite fearless in other ways can be terribly phobic of a specific situation. A woman in her fifties came to see me just before a planned airplane flight from New York to Florida. She is an M.D., a pediatric surgeon, and the mother of two teenaged children. She was certainly used to the high-tension atmosphere of an operating room, and was known for her cool competency even under the pressure of surgical emergencies. Nothing seemed to scare her—at least not in the operating room. She had reserved a flight for herself and her kids, scheduled for a date one week from our meeting. She'd often taken these trips before, and each time a few days before the flight, she became preoccupied with fears and anxiety. Driving to the airport, she would have intrusive images of the plane crashing, a profound sense of everything being out of control; sometimes physical symptoms—specifically episodes of vomiting—would precede the ride to the airport. Once the plane landed, she felt better, and then a few days before returning home, the whole process would start again. She had come to see me because the feelings were returning, and she knew she needed help. This was not a person who feared the evaluation or judgment of others. She didn't even fear situations that would scare me (and I think most people) half to death—like a surgical emergency with a child. This woman certainly did not have social anxiety, but rather a specific phobia: fear of flying in airplanes.

People with agoraphobia, for example, feel panicked in public situations where escape may be difficult, but the reasons for their fear are quite different from those of people with social anxiety. A person with agoraphobia may feel panicked when riding in a train. He senses that he is trapped, unable to escape, and these panicky feelings, with all the physiological accompaniments of increased heart rate, sweating, flushing, and so on begin to overtake him. In other words, he is starting to have a panic attack. The exact same feelings, with the same unpleasant physiological symptoms, may be experienced by a person with social anxiety sitting next to him, but the person with social anxiety doesn't fear entrapment with no escape— instead, he fears that he will be humiliated by other people in the train noticing his growing panic. Same feeling, different cause. And since the treatments for the two disorders are also different, I have to make sure I know what the reasons for the fear and panic really are before I decide what will help. A certain kind of question can help make this distinction. I might ask a fearful patient, "Would it frighten you to walk through a train station if you could be sure that you didn't have to talk to anyone on your way through?" If the patient says, "Yes, I'd be afraid," then my suspicion is that agoraphobia, and not social anxiety is the problem. If the patient says, "No, just walking through without anyone getting a chance to notice me or having to talk to anyone wouldn't really bother me," then the problem she's suffering from is more likely social anxiety, and I would pursue that hint with more discussion to make sure.

If a patient comes to me with the complaint of a specific fear—the fear of spiders, let's say—I'll want to know more about what else she fears and what else troubles her. But unless I can isolate the fear of social interactions—and be convinced that the focus is on the fear of a negative evaluation by others in those public situations—I won't conclude that social anxiety is the problem. If a person's only "social" fear is that of giving a speech to a large audience, and if this is his only fear about showing himself in public, I will be hesitant to diagnose social anxiety. The fears of a person with social anxiety are generalized to all, or almost all, social or public situations. Making this distinction is not just an idle academic exercise. The diagnosis will determine the treatment, and the treatments for social anxiety and specific phobia are not the same. Pharmacological treatments, for example, are ineffective for specific phobias, but they work quite well, as we will discuss later in this book, for social anxiety. Getting the diagnosis right is essential.

Panic Attacks

Even though panic attack is a separate disorder, panic attacks are sometimes associated with social anxiety disorder. This was the case with Carlos, a thirty-five-year-old salesman for a pharmaceutical company—a "detail man" as they're called. Although I'd never met him, he did come to our hospital to call on doctors and show his wares, and one of my colleagues referred him to me. He seemed to me perfectly well put-together, looking pretty much like any other detail man you'd see around the hospital, well dressed and well spoken. But he wasn't in my office to sell pharmaceuticals. His problem, he told me, was that every once in a while he'd suddenly start to feel a rapidly growing fear, a feeling of loss of control, a terror of going crazy or dying. Sometimes he thought he was having a heart attack or a stroke, and in discussing this with him, I learned that these attacks were not just out of the blue, but specifically occurred in settings where he felt he was being judged or evaluated and where falling short might mean rejection or humiliation. The first one occurred when he was giving a talk for his job—sitting right in a doctor's office, he panicked. At one point in his presentation, he suddenly couldn't think what to say next, completely focused as he was on how the doctor might be evaluating his performance. He began having physical symptoms—increased heartbeat, sweating—that quickly escalated into a panic attack. Yet unlike a classic panic attack, which can occur with no apparent provocation at all, this only happened to him when he was forced to perform in some way. It never occurred in the subway or on bridges; it never woke him up at night the way panic attacks can and do. The panic attacks were in some sense a symptom of his social anxiety.

Social Anxiety That Doesn't Need Treatment

What if a person is afraid of, say, public speaking, but never has any occasion to speak in public, and his fear doesn't interfere in any way with his everyday functioning? Is such a person still suffering from social anxiety and in need of treatment? Probably not. It could be that a person with generalized social anxiety avoids situations where he has to speak in public—avoidance protects him, but that doesn't mean he doesn't have social anxiety, or that he isn't functioning at a level well below his potential. On the other hand, a housewife who goes to parties, interacts with people at school, doesn't have any anxiety may be a person with a specific form of performance anxiety who isn't bothered by it because the specific situation she fears never really comes up. I don't believe there is any reason to treat such a person.

Social Anxiety, or Just Plain Shyness?

People with social anxiety, unlike those who are simply shy, spend inordinate amounts of time thinking negative thoughts in anticipation of their performance in public situations. Often the anxiety simply makes a person avoid the public event completely. A woman with social anxiety may manage to follow through with a public performance, but she imagines only the worst: I talked too fast, I mumbled, I spoke too loudly, I made mistakes, I made a fool of myself. These thoughts persist after the event as the woman goes over the details repeatedly, concentrating on failures real or imagined, reliving the shame, thinking about the negative consequences of the poor performance, even recalling other moments of perceived public humiliation to reinforce her belief in her inadequacy. Errors invisible to everyone in the audience take vivid shape in her mind. She's not just shy—she's overwhelmingly anxious.

The kind of social anxiety that can affect performance on an academic test, for example, bears little resemblance to ordinary shyness, and few would confuse the two. Taking a test provokes at least some degree of anxiety in almost all of us, and those with social anxiety are even more likely to be beset with fears of performance and the terror of failure in this situation. There is plenty of evidence to connect this kind of excessive anxiety with poor academic performance, and this is not surprising—anxiety interferes with the performance of all kinds of tasks that involve cognitive ability. Some interesting research

❖ FINAL EXAM

I once saw a man in his fifties who had been working quite successfully as a chef in one of Manhattan's fancier restaurants. He'd even written and published a cookbook that turned out to be quite successful. When his two kids graduated from college and were pretty much out on their own, he decided to follow an old dream: he went back to school to become a psychologist. Even though he was pretty rusty in academic matters, he quickly caught on again, did well in class, participated in discussions with enthusiasm and intelligence, and even did a presentation on childhood IQ tests that garnered high praise from his dour and demanding teacher in a course on psychological testing methods. Shy, he was not. Indeed, he was quite outgoing, even with classmates he'd just met. But every time there was an exam, he would have an overwhelming fear of not performing well. Just the announcement or scheduling of an exam would make him start to sweat. It wasn't a fear of not knowing the material—rationally, he knew that he'd studied hard and had a good grasp of everything that was going on in the class and in assigned reading. But whatever rational thoughts he had about his fears, he was completely unable to put them aside, and often wound up just skipping exams entirely. Needless to say, this did not help his grade-point average, and he had to drop out of school. This made him depressed and remorseful even as it freed him of the anxiety that had made him flee in the first place. There was, eventually, a happy ending—with therapy and medicine he was able to return to school—but the point is that this congenial and outgoing man suffered from an anxiety that was extremely destructive.

on this subject suggests that it is the mental state of anxiety itself—not the physical effects of the mental state like increased heartbeat or sweating—that harms performance. That is, the worrying in a sense takes up space in the mind that would otherwise be devoted to getting the right answers. In fact, anxiety seems to have less effect on the performance of physical tasks than mental tasks.

Shyness is a personality characteristic. Social anxiety is a psychiatric disorder. This formulation, while not inaccurate, disguises the complexity of the problem. The factors that produce shyness—temperament, family, socialization, and self-esteem—are common to both ordinary bashfulness and social anxiety disorder, which sometimes makes the distinction unclear. The difference is important because it will help me determine the treatment. In general, when I see a patient whose bashfulness seriously disrupts the pursuit of ordinary daily activities causing extreme disruptions in his life, I look for social anxiety as the cause.

Shyness and Social Anxiety at the Same Time

Shyness and social anxiety often overlap in the same person. Distinguishing them is important for many reasons, not the least of which is to answer the now common charge that mental health professionals are "medicalizing" an ordinary personality trait in order to treat it as a disease. An interesting recent study helps to clarify this issue. The subjects were undergraduate psychology students at San Diego State University. More than 2,000 students participated, and each filled out a well-tested shyness screening questionnaire called the Revised Cheek and Buss Shyness Scale. Then the researchers took the 10 percent of students who scored highest on the test—that is, those who were the shyest—and compared them to the group that scored in the 40th to 50th percentile, those average in shyness. Without knowing which students were in which group, researchers examined the 303 students (the two groups were similar in ethnic background and gender distribution) to find out which of them suffered from the symptoms of social anxiety disorder. The findings were dramatic: 18 percent of the average shyness group had SAD, while 49 percent of the highly shy group had that diagnosis. There were, by a wide margin, more people in the highly shy group who had generalized social anxiety, the more severe and debilitating form of the disease. Moreover, highly shy people with social anxiety were significantly more impaired in social functioning than highly shy people without the diagnosis. Shyness is not a psychiatric disorder, social anxiety is.

Shyness is a transitory condition; social anxiety is chronic—untreated it can last a lifetime. Shyness is not incapacitating; social anxiety often is. Other researchers set out to determine systematically the differences between them by studying a group of 200 undergraduates at the University of Maryland. First they used a questionnaire (the Revised Cheek and Buss Shyness Scale) to divide the subjects into shy and not shy groups. Then they interviewed the students to determine which had a diagnosis of social anxiety and which did not. Shyness was normally distributed in the sample, and there was no significant difference in the gender of the shy and not shy students. Among the shy students, 17.7 percent met the criteria for a diagnosis of social anxiety. But among the not shy, only 2.9 percent could be diagnosed as socially anxious. So though most socially anxious students were shy, they were nevertheless a small minority of the shy group. The results did show a correlation between severe shyness and social anxiety, but the students with social anxiety could not be characterized as merely "extremely shy."

The shy students were much more likely to have other psychiatric diagnoses than the not shy, outranking them in mood disorders, substance use disorders, and personality disorders of various kinds. In fact, two-thirds of the shy students had a psychiatric diagnosis.

We'll have more to say about this in chapter 4, but it is enough to say for the moment that social anxiety is often accompanied by other psychiatric problems.

Social Anxiety and Self-Worth

The person suffering from social anxiety views his "shyness" as not just a poor performance on a single occasion, but a reflection of a profound inadequacy and a confirmation that "other people will not like me, will view me as stupid, and will reject me—and no wonder: I'm a worthless failure. Who could like a nerd like me?" Some people with social anxiety will say that they don't have such thoughts when they are with their families or close friends, but only where they think some stranger may be evaluating their performance. Usually, the anxiety decreases rapidly with the end of the public performance. In rare and extreme cases, though, the thoughts can be so painful that they lead to profound depression and even suicide.

ॐ

Many people described as "shy" grow out of their shyness—non-shy adults often describe themselves as having been shy children or teenagers. But people who have social anxiety have an unremitting disease that they almost never grow out of without treatment. How does a mental health professional decide if you have social anxiety instead of some other disease or no disease at all? As in diagnosing any disorder, the doctor looks for symptoms. It is these symptoms that we'll discuss next.

Symptoms

You are an expert in how you feel, and that's why your collaboration is absolutely essential to treating social anxiety. When I first meet a patient, I conduct an interview. This isn't an interrogation—I don't sit there with a clipboard reading a list of questions and marking down the answers; I don't even have a list of questions in mind (although I did when I was first starting out). I want to find out who, what, and when, but I stay away from asking why.

Your Feelings, and What the Doctor Makes of Them

You feel very shy, sometimes even a little scared. Your heart beats faster when you think about giving a speech in public, and when the time comes to actually perform, you start to sweat and pace. But does this mean you have social anxiety and need medicine or psychotherapy to "cure" it? Not necessarily. The diagnosis of social anxiety, like that of many other psychiatric disorders, depends on a combination of the patient's own testimony and the knowledge and experience of the diagnosing physician. This requires a degree of cooperation from the patient that isn't required in diagnosing, say, an infectious disease for which there is a laboratory test.

Deciding when social anxiety should be treated—like deciding when high blood pressure should be treated—can sometimes be a judgment call. Like high blood pressure and many other disorders, social anxiety has a range of severity, and no two cases are exactly alike. It is a strange fact that many people with social anxiety do not even consider themselves "shy" in the ordinary sense of that word. Often they don't seem shy to others, either. They can and do appear as perfectly normal, not particularly anxious or nervous or obviously withdrawn. The distress can be well hidden, and their avoidance of the feared situations so thorough that even those close to them fail to realize how profoundly they are suffering.

Depression

Often patients come into treatment for comorbid problems like depression and don't immediately volunteer their fears of social situations and their attempts to avoid them. A woman came to me for treatment whose symptoms certainly looked like depression. Janet, as I'll call her, a thirty-five-year-old stockbroker, lived with her lawyer husband in one of those giant new houses they're building in suburbs these days—the kind with 10,000 square feet of living space and a 4-car garage. I couldn't imagine what they did with all that space, since they had no kids, but let's just say that they were, to put it mildly, living large. I have a suspicion that money, contrary to popular belief, can sometimes actually buy happiness, but in this case it surely hadn't. Janet had completely lost interest in the house she had been enthusiastically decorating, didn't have any close friends, and reported that "I'm just too tired when I get home, and everything seems gray. I wake up in the morning with a sinking feeling in my stomach at the prospect of getting up and going to work." Fifteen minutes of conversation like this, and it was obvious to me that she was depressed. But it was only after a long discussion of her depressed feelings that I learned she also had a profound dread of social interactions—which is not a symptom of depression at all. Calling people on the phone or meeting with clients—and these were requirements of her job and at times impossible to avoid— terrified her, and she had all she could do to keep her fears to herself, hidden from her coworkers and boss. She was making plenty of money, but despite her success she hadn't risen in her firm, partly because that would have made her face even greater social challenges that she was desperate to avoid. She undoubtedly needed help with her depression, but that's not what was interfering with her progress in her career. The fault for that lay in her social anxiety.

The Medical Definition of Social Anxiety

There are specific criteria to be met—symptoms that have to be observed—before a doctor will make a diagnosis of social anxiety, just as there are specific criteria that have to be met to make a diagnosis of physical illnesses.

The *Diagnostic and Statistical Manual,* fourth edition (*DSM-IV*), outlines the conditions that justify a diagnosis of social anxiety.* Here's what it says:

Diagnostic Criteria for Social Phobia

A. A marked and persistent fear of one or more social or performance situations in which the person is exposed to unfamiliar

Diagnostic and Statistical Manual of Mental Disorders, 4th Edition. Washington, D.C.: American Psychiatric Association, 1994. Used by permission.

people or to possible scrutiny by others. The individual fears that he or she will act in a way (or show anxiety symptoms) that will be humiliating or embarrassing. Note: In children, there must be evidence of the capacity for age-appropriate social relationships with familiar people and the anxiety must occur in peer settings, not just in interactions with adults.

B. Exposure to the feared social situation almost invariably provokes anxiety, which may take the form of a situationally bound or situationally predisposed Panic Attack. Note: In children, the anxiety may be expressed by crying, tantrums, freezing, or shrinking from social situations with unfamiliar people.

C. The person recognizes that the fear is excessive or unreasonable. Note: In children, this feature may be absent.

D. The feared social or performance situations are avoided or else are endured with intense anxiety or distress.

E. The avoidance, anxious anticipation, or distress in the feared social or performance situation(s) interferes significantly with the person's normal routine, occupational (academic) functioning, or social activities or relationships, or there is marked distress about having the phobia.

F. In individuals under age 18 years, the duration is at least 6 months.

G. The fear or avoidance is not due to the direct physiological effects of a substance (e.g., a drug of abuse, a medication) or a general medical condition and is not better accounted for by another mental disorder (e.g., Panic Disorder With or Without Agoraphobia, Separation Anxiety Disorder, Body Dysmorphic Disorder, a Pervasive Developmental Disorder, or Schizoid Personality Disorder).

H. If a general medical condition or another mental disorder is present, the fear in Criterion A is unrelated to it, e.g., the fear is not of Stuttering, trembling in Parkinson's disease, or exhibiting abnormal eating behavior in Anorexia Nervosa or Bulimia Nervosa.

Specify if:
Generalized: if the fears include most social situations (also consider the additional diagnosis of Avoidant Personality Disorder).

That last instruction needs some explaining. It is generally recognized that there are two subtypes of social anxiety, specific (sometimes called nongeneralized or discrete) and generalized. With specific social phobia, only one or two activities provoke anxiety; in generalized social phobia almost all social interactions produce panic and physiological symptoms. Most patients who go into treatment for social anxiety suffer from the generalized form. The two subtypes differ not just in the number of fears, but also in their heritability, comorbidity with other illnesses, and the degree of impairment they produce. The distinction is important, because the two subtypes respond to different kinds of treatment.

There are also rating scales designed for finding out if a person has social anxiety, used more in research projects than in actual diagnosis with individual patients, but these are not like the questionnaires used in psychiatric diagnosis and not like the "test your personality" questionnaires published in popular magazines. These scales are tested with many practitioners and patients to be sure that they can be used consistently and that they are consistent when different therapists fill them out with the same person, and when the same person fills them out at different times. They are tested before and after treatment, to see if treatment changes the rating in a given patient. The tests and studies that examine these scales involve complex statistical techniques and theories, which we don't need to go into here—it is enough to say that these rating scales are not arrived at casually or arbitrarily.

Age and Social Anxiety

It's rare that anyone past the age of twenty-five or so would suddenly come down with social anxiety. Occasionally, someone with the disease will be thrust into a situation in which it becomes evident—say, a promotion to a job that entails a lot of public speaking. Suddenly, the person realizes that public speaking, which had never before played any role in his or her life, has become an essential everyday task, and that the debilitating fear it provokes has become an insurmountable barrier to performing it successfully. But social anxiety generally appears in the teenage years or early twenties. People recover much more easily without treatment from specific social phobia. It arises, like the generalized subtype, in adolescence and, although its course can be quite long, it often disappears on its own. This isn't true of the generalized subtype, which is much more likely to run in families than the nongeneralized, and people with the generalized subtype are much more likely to have other psychiatric illnesses along with their social anxiety. About two-thirds of those with social anxiety suffer with the more debilitating generalized version.

"They All Think I'm an Idiot!": How People with Social Anxiety View Themselves

People with social anxiety have negative thoughts that are not based on any actual expression of opinion from those who hear or see them in public places. These patients don't care what you say—they're convinced they're boring, awkward, foolish, or ridiculous without any outside evidence, even in the face of assertions to the contrary by acquaintances, friends, family, and therapists eager to help them. Telling them that they are not what they are already firmly convinced they actually are does not help. They vastly overestimate the degree to which others notice their anxiety, assuming that it is as obvious to others as it is to themselves. This is not just a hunch—studies have shown that people with social anxiety rate their own behavior much more negatively than independent observers do.

In many cases, there is a "self-fulfilling prophecy" effect of this kind of behavior. Believing a person dislikes you affects the way you present yourself—this is as true of people who don't suffer from social anxiety as of those who do. People who suffer from social anxiety, however, concentrate extremely hard on the impression they're making, convinced that that impression, whatever they do, will be negative. This intense attention focused on themselves does often leave a negative impression on others, reinforcing the socially anxious person's belief in his own inadequacy.

Socially anxious people believe that their (imagined) poor performance makes them the center of attention in any social situation. Everyone is looking at them, noticing every defect, criticizing silently. When a socially anxious person thinks back on her performance, she concentrates exclusively on the negative aspects: "I hesitated and stuttered. I lost track of what I was saying. I made awkward hand gestures that everyone noticed. They all think I'm an idiot." This kind of "post-event processing" reinforces all the negative beliefs she already holds, helping to set those beliefs firmly in concrete, providing "proof" that she is in fact a social failure. All this, as we will see later in this book, has implications for the treatment of the disorder.

Public Speaking

Fearing public speaking is probably the most common symptom of social anxiety. Public speaking makes everyone anxious to some degree, but it completely paralyzes those who suffer from social anxiety. This problem affects people in all walks of life, and at all levels of achievement. A professor of medicine I know had achieved notable success in his research and publications but had studiously avoided going to any conference where he would have to present his work in person—practically a necessity for anyone involved in the world of scientific research. The idea simply terrified him. He understood his problem and had undergone various treatments for it, but none had been successful. Then, spontaneously, after twenty years of avoiding lectures or presentations outside his own institution, he had a complete remission of symptoms and was able to go on a lecture tour, during which many others in the field met him for the first time. He actually thought his ailment helped him by allowing him to focus on his work without the distractions of travel and the social interaction of scientific meetings. Did his treatments finally take effect? Did his problem just go away by itself? Although true social anxiety rarely disappears on its own, there's really no way of knowing exactly what happened in this doctor's case. But I suppose it can be said that in some cases, at least, fear of public speaking can have its positive side.

Shy Bladder Syndrome

Fear of urinating in a public bathroom can create enormous problems, and it is a common symptom of social anxiety. This is sometimes called "shy bladder syndrome," and the medical term for it is paruresis. In some cases it can lead to serious medical complications. Some patients manage to keep the problem secret for years, carefully avoiding any situation in which they will be forced to use a public bathroom. A thirty-five-year-old patient of mine was unable to use urinals in public restrooms and could only urinate if he was sitting down in the toilet stall. Even hidden in the stall, he couldn't urinate if someone else was in the room. He was fearful of being scrutinized, having his genitals compared to those of other men, fearful that his might be judged inferior. The problem was so persistent that he eventually developed bladder problems. I treated this person very slowly. First I gave him Effexor XR in doses of 15 milligrams a day, and after about five weeks of medication, I encouraged him to go to the public restroom at his workplace and to urinate sitting in the stall while someone else was in the bathroom. For the first time, he was able to do it. We then set up a program that had him first urinate at a urinal when no one else was in the bathroom, then when someone was there but not using the urinal next to him, and finally when someone was standing right next to him as he urinated. When his thoughts drifted toward the person next to him, he was encouraged to refocus his attention on the urination rather than being scrutinized by others. For someone who has never suffered from this syndrome, or has never heard of it, there may be something slightly comical in it. But I can assure you that for those who have the problem, there's nothing amusing about it. Ridding himself of these fears actually improved his general demeanor in the workplace, leading to happier, more satisfying, and more successful work.

Talking on the Telephone

With cell phone conversations now interfering with almost every human activity, from watching a movie to riding on a train, it may be hard to believe that some people are incapable of making a phone call in public. Yet this is exactly what a person with SAD can face, and it leads to serious practical problems. One patient of mine, a young woman coming home from college, missed the train she was supposed to catch to make it home in time for Thanksgiving dinner. Having the sense that she was being observed by others in the busy station, she found it impossible to go to a public phone and call her family. Even thinking of having to make the call made her nauseated. She told me the story with a smile and a shake of her head at what she perceived as her "weakness," but she knew that she had left her family wondering what had become of her. This was not weakness, of course, but one of the many destructive symptoms of social anxiety.

Returning Merchandise to a Store

Returning goods to a store is a routine chore for most people, but for the socially anxious, it is agony. A high school student I met with had to buy some poster board to do a class presentation. Discovering that he'd bought the wrong color or size (I can't remember exactly which now), he was told to go back to the store to exchange it for the appropriate material—a simple enough task for most people. But not for him. His first thought was that the store clerk would think him indecisive, uninformed, even stupid. This was enough to terrify him. He wound up buying entirely new material rather than go through the torture of exchanging the old stuff. Social anxiety can have its economic burdens as well—and I assure you that those burdens can be considerably larger than this young man's in this situation.

Small Groups

Participating in small groups or speaking up in meetings is impossible for many with social anxiety. It is easy to imagine how debilitating such a problem can be for anyone who works in an organization that demands interaction with others in just such situations. This is a symptom of social anxiety that can actually destroy a career before it even gets started. Hardly anyone sympathizes with or understands the problem of a person who has nothing to add to the meeting—they just assume he's stupid, or at best lacking in imagination, devoid of ideas. This is no way to make a good impression on the boss.

Writing in Public

Some socially anxious people can't work or write with others watching. This isn't just a harmless quirk—it can be another serious obstacle to career success. For some, even signing a check or a credit card slip in front of others is impossible. This was the affliction presented to me by a thirty-eight-year-old mother of two small children. On checking out in the supermarket, she is unable to pay for her purchases either with a check or credit card because the tremor in her hand is so severe that her signature would be indecipherable. She worries that the salesclerk and others on line will notice her anxiety, judge her, and find her lacking. She solves the problem by making sure she always has enough cash at the food store, but larger purchases of more expensive items, or other situations that require signing a credit card receipt, are virtually impossible. She studiously avoids such tasks as applying for a bank loan, initialing a sales contract, renting a car, or performing any other task that requires writing in public. Routine tasks that most people take for granted are for her insuperable obstacles. In other words, this disease interferes with ordinary ways of negotiating the world, making everything in her life more difficult.

❖ AT LAST: A GOOD BOSS

One of my patients is a twenty-three-year-old woman who graduated two years ago from an Ivy League college. She majored in history with a minor in biology, and had been accepted at a medical school, but she wanted to take some time off, so she deferred her studies. She has an interesting and rewarding job working as a research coordinator in the neurology department of a large academic medical center. Every week she attends a department-wide meeting of researchers where she has to discuss issues concerning recruitment of subjects, lab space assignments, the progress of various studies, and so on—all of the problems and issues that have arisen during the previous week. During these meetings, her mind would go blank, she would stutter, sweat, and blush, completely lose track of her thoughts, unable to recover even by resorting to reading her notes. Fortunately for her, she has a perceptive boss. He knew she was intelligent, well organized, and competent, and he could see that there was something serious standing in the way of her performing properly. She was able to talk with her boss about this problem (this was not easy for her and I admired her courage), and he wisely pushed her to seek treatment. Medicine was extremely effective in her case. I suggested she take a beta-blocker, atanolol, one hour before her meeting. It didn't work immediately—there are no miracle cures, at least not in my experience—but she was able, after a couple of meetings, to see her symptoms disappear and perform properly, without any of the emotional or physical symptoms of anxiety.

Shame and Panic

The overwhelming emotion of people with social anxiety is shame. A person's sense of shame may be realistic or not, but for a socially anxious person it is nevertheless the overriding concern. He feels shame from a depreciated public image caused by others observing him violating social norms. His failure to conform to these social norms, he feels, makes him inferior, inept, immature, even stupid. The only solution he sees is to conceal or avoid the shameful behavior, but at the same time he feels incapable of concealing the shame when forced into the public situations that upset him. He is convinced that ridicule, derision, contempt, and disparagement are the reactions he will inevitably provoke in others as soon as they see him in one of the situations he fears. It isn't just a crowd of people who will feel this way—the salesperson in the store or the faceless person on the telephone can provoke the same feelings of shame. This feeling is different from anxiety. Anxiety disappears after the event is over; shame persists indefinitely.

Panic attacks often accompany social anxiety, but panic attacks by themselves are not an indication of the disease. Panic disorder and social anxiety disorder are two distinct illnesses. In fact, the panic associated with social anxiety is both cognitively and symptomatically different from that experienced in panic disorder. Patients with panic disorder are more likely to experience their feelings as unconnected to any particular impending event—the attack is spontaneous. Those with social anxiety disorder, on the other hand, have a feeling of panic that almost always centers around the fear of the particular social interaction they are about to face—speaking in front of an audience, for example. Although many of the physical symptoms of patients with panic disorder and those with social anxiety overlap—blushing, sweating, increased heart rate—people with panic disorder are more likely to feel dizziness, faintness, and numbness than are those with social anxiety.

Panic disorder and social anxiety disorder often exist together—two studies suggest that about half of patients with social phobia also have panic disorder. Even in these cases, the social anxiety usually comes first, with the panic disorder following when the patient is older. A teenaged girl, shy and inhibited, came into my office to discuss her panic attacks, for which she had been diagnosed some time ago. She was seventeen, but looked younger, barely five feet tall with her brown hair tied back in a short ponytail. Most seventeen-year-old girls dress in a way that suggests they're trying to look older and more sophisticated than they really are. There was no suggestion of such affectations in this girl. Her voice was that of a younger child as well, the kind kids use in addressing an intimidating adult. As I spoke with her, gathering a medical and psychiatric history, I learned that her fears of social interaction developed early in childhood. In fact, her problem was so severe that it led to her dropping out of high school to be home schooled. Social situations surely caused her considerable distress early on, but later simply going out of the house could provoke panic. In this young woman's case, the age of onset and the pervasive quality of the fear made it evident that the primary problem was not panic disorder but social anxiety. After the social anxiety, other problems follow. Treating the panic disorder and ignoring the social anxiety would have been a major mistake.

The age at which the disorders first occur is another clue to their difference. Social anxiety disorder almost always begins in adolescence, often early adolescence. Panic disorder, on the other hand, typically has its first onset when the patient is in the mid-twenties or even later. Moreover, the panic attacks of panic disorder often send people to the emergency room—they think they're in serious physical trouble, maybe even dying, and are eager for treatment. People with social phobia don't usually show up in emergency rooms, even when their panic is severe.

~~

Distinguishing the symptoms of social anxiety from those of other diseases and disorders is essential to proper treatment. This is especially important because social anxiety is so often accompanied by other illnesses.

More Than One Illness

It is uncommon for social anxiety to be the only reason a person comes to see me. Usually, social anxiety is accompanied by other psychiatric illnesses, often other anxiety disorders, and when it is, I want to treat those illnesses as well. Studies show that somewhere between 50 and 80 percent of people with SAD also have another psychiatric diagnosis.

Patients with social anxiety accompanied by other psychiatric illnesses are more likely to feel impaired, more likely to report that their illness interferes with their lives, more likely to have received treatment from a mental health specialist, and more likely to have taken medication for their illness. Panic disorder, obsessive-compulsive disorder, and depression are common accompaniments of social anxiety, and, according to some studies, eating disorders also often accompany SAD. These high rates of comorbidity are not apparent in other anxiety disorders. While one-third of patients with SAD have more than one other anxiety disorder, only 16 percent of people with panic disorder do. Clearly, social anxiety predisposes people to other mental illnesses, and it is associated with more malignant varieties of those illnesses as well.

Major depression and bipolar illness are the greatest dangers, since they can be fatal illnesses, and the most severe kinds of social anxiety are the most likely to be accompanied by depression. Patients with bipolar illness may be the most difficult to treat, because many of the medications for social anxiety disorder can exacerbate bipolar symptoms. When the bipolar illness worsens, so does accompanying anxiety.

Although social anxiety by itself is probably not a risk for suicide attempts, people with social anxiety and comorbid depression are more than fifteen times as likely to attempt suicide as those with social anxiety alone. In a large study of more than 13,000 adults, researchers found that major disorders were comorbid in 69 percent of people with social anxiety, and that social anxiety was associated with increased thoughts of suicide, increased financial dependency, and increased number of visits to health care facilities. Yet the study also found that social anxiety was rarely treated by mental health professionals. Given the results of studies like this one, the early detection of social anxiety seems essential, and health care professionals should be aware that other mental illnesses are likely to be present as well. If a patient with major depression is treated only for a complaint of social anxiety, the therapist is making a mistake of gargantuan proportions.

SAD and Depression

These are not easy diagnoses to make, and they can considerably complicate treatment plans. A person who has depression and social anxiety may find relief from the social anxiety treatment if he takes benzodiazepine, but that same medicine could make the accompanying depression worse. A patient with SAD and comorbid alcohol abuse, given benzodiazepine for the social anxiety, may make the alcoholism more severe, or leave him dependent on the drug. These are specific examples of how comorbid conditions influence treatment choice, and the therapist who is not knowledgeable about and looking out for these things isn't doing his or her job.

Early treatment of social anxiety can almost certainly help avoid later problems with other psychiatric ailments. One adolescent patient who had suffered untreated social anxiety disorder in childhood came to see me after a suicide attempt. She'd been pretty much an outsider throughout her high school years, and although she'd graduated and been accepted at an out-of-state college, she was unable to enroll. She now had a low-wage job well beneath her capabilities. It didn't take long before I concluded that she was clearly suffering from major depression. But I was convinced that early treatment of her social anxiety would have helped her later avoid the more serious problem that now overlaid her social anxiety. On the other hand, another of my patients with the same kind of early social anxiety had parents who were sensitive to the symptoms and got intervention early, both psychotherapy and medication. As a result, her symptoms improved, and she managed to go on to college, graduate school, and a professional career, untouched by secondary anxiety or depressive symptoms. My experience with these two patients is not a scientific experiment, and it doesn't prove anything. After all, the second patient may never have experienced depression anyway. But early intervention may have saved her from developing secondary problems, and even if it didn't, the early treatment certainly saved her from the considerable pain of persistent social anxiety.

Social anxiety and depression may be connected in other ways as well. Several studies have demonstrated a link between social anxiety and the early onset of major depression. Studies have also found that youngsters with social anxiety have more severe kinds of depression, more protracted episodes, more suicidal ideation, and more suicide attempts than depressed people without the comorbid illness. It is these kinds of observations that make me strongly suspect, even if I can't prove it, that treating social anxiety in children might reduce the risk for depression as they grow older.

Alcohol Use and Abuse

Alcoholism is about twice as common in people with social anxiety as in otherwise healthy people. It is probably no surprise to anyone that alcohol is used, even by people who do not suffer from social anxiety, to make social interactions easier and more pleasant. That's why they serve cocktails at parties. Many social anxiety patients report using alcohol specifically to help them face social situations that they otherwise find intolerable. Alcohol or illicit drugs may also be used as self-medication to treat the unpleasant feelings of loneliness and social isolation that result from social anxiety. These are, of course, completely ineffective treatments and can be dangerous as well.

Aside from totally avoiding social situations, using alcohol is probably the most common way people cope with their social anxiety. It isn't clear whether alcohol has a genuine stress-reducing property or whether it is the mere expectation that alcohol will help that makes people with social anxiety use it. In any case, if alcohol seems to work the first time, SAD sufferers will use it again and again. Some of these people will develop alcoholism. An even larger number will suffer the other consequences of excessive drinking: car accidents and other physical trauma, medical risks, and interpersonal problems.

Estimates vary considerably, but most studies report rates of alcoholism among social anxiety patients at between 14 and 40 percent. This compares with a rate in the general population of 9 to 14 percent. Unfortunately, alcohol can also increase anxiety, and the socially anxious person who uses it can become trapped in a vicious circle, drinking to relieve the anxiety (which works for a while) and then increasing the drinking to relieve the anxiety that the drinking itself is provoking. To make matters more complicated, the anxiety caused by alcohol can be difficult for a doctor to distinguish from the anxiety produced by social anxiety disorder, making diagnosis and treatment more problematic.

Alcohol use complicates treatment in other ways as well. MAO inhibitors (drugs such as Nardil, Parnate, Marplan, and Eldepryl) cannot be used with people who drink beer or wine. These drugs have a potentially fatal reaction not with the alcohol itself, but with the enzymes in any fermented foods or drinks. Benzodiazepines are dangerous when taken with any alcohol (see chapter 10 for more on these drugs). The usual kinds of psychotherapy used to treat SAD may be ineffective with heavy drinkers. Conversely, social anxiety makes the treatment of alcoholism more difficult. For example, people with SAD are likely to resist group therapy or self-help meetings like Alcoholics Anonymous. We'll have more to say about the psychological and pharmacological treatments for SAD in chapters 10 and 11, but for the moment let me say this: heavy alcohol use is unhealthy, and particularly so for people with social anxiety.

❖ SOCIAL DRINKING?
OR SOCIAL ANXIETY DRINKING?

Jim was a twenty-three-year-old recent college graduate unsure of what kind of career he wanted to pursue. There's nothing unusual, and certainly nothing psychiatrically abnormal, about being twenty-three and not knowing exactly where you're going in life, but this young man arrived in my office at the urging of friends who felt his alcohol consumption was getting out of control. At first meeting, he seemed a perfectly normal-looking, well-turned-out twenty-three-year-old—the two-day growth of beard he sported was clearly a fashion statement, not evidence that he was neglecting his personal grooming. He'd been a sociology major in college but couldn't find work that really interested him. He had started in a sales position at a company that sold electrical equipment for use in industry and large buildings but found it too stressful, and wound up working in a back-office job in the same company. His work didn't engage him, and he searched for life's satisfactions elsewhere. He told me in great detail of his adventures with high school friends, going to bars to pick up women, and always drinking heavily in the process. I told him I understood why he'd want to get his mind off a job that was at best uninspiring, but I suggested that going out with his friends, and especially trying to pick up girls, might be completely impossible for him without the help of alcohol. He admitted that there was some truth to this—when sober, he conceded, he was pretty shy and self-contained. Drinking made things "a hell of a lot easier." While he was eager to meet women, his anxiety about it was overwhelming, and only heavy drinking allowed him to join in the social activities. In fact, alcohol had become the solution not only to picking up girls, but to many other anxiety-provoking situations as well. Eventually it got so bad that he was having blackouts, not remembering what happened the night before, and suffering from crippling hangovers. Alcohol had become his treatment of choice for social anxiety, and it was clearly not an effective one. Whenever I see a young man abusing alcohol, I want to know if there is an underlying social anxiety disorder—it's often there beneath the substance abuse. Men with social anxiety are more likely to succumb to alcoholism than are women with the same disorder (and alcoholism in general is more common in men than in women).

Usually, social anxiety, which begins in adolescence, precedes alcoholism, unlike the situation with generalized anxiety, which usually comes after alcohol dependence has already begun. This is true of other comorbid disorders as well. In a large majority of cases, social anxiety occurs before mood disorders, other anxiety disorders, and substance abuse disorders. In one large study, researchers found that in socially anxious people with other psychiatric illnesses, the social phobia preceded 85.2 percent of substance use disorders, 81.6 percent of depressive disorders, and 64.4 percent of the other anxiety disorders. The only comorbid illness that seemed to have an earlier age of onset than social anxiety was specific phobia. We can't jump to conclusions here—that social anxiety precedes these other illnesses doesn't mean it causes them. But it is almost certainly true that social anxiety is a predictor of future psychiatric illness, and it is likely that the demoralization, social isolation, and friendlessness caused by SAD also contribute to a tendency toward depression.

Smoking

Smoking—probably the biggest single cause of preventable illness in the United States—is also more common in adolescents who suffer from social anxiety. Although youngsters with social anxiety, on average, start smoking later than their smoking peers, they smoke more and become nicotine dependent more often and more rapidly. As with other kinds of drugs, kids may use nicotine to allay anxiety. In other words, social anxiety can and does lead people to take up a deadly habit.

What effect might treating social anxiety have on drug abuse? The World Health Organization's International Consortium in Psychiatric Epidemiology did a large international study to try to figure this out. Carried out in North America, Latin America, and Europe, the details depend on complex statistical analyses, but it is enough here to report the results: between 17.5 and 25.9 percent of all drug dependence could be prevented by treating social anxiety early.

Physical Illness

A recently published paper suggests that people who are excessively shy may be more susceptible to infectious diseases as well. Researchers at the University of California at Los Angeles found that HIV-infected men who were rated highest for social inhibition carried viral loads as much as ten times greater than those who were not shy, and benefited less from treatment with antiretroviral drugs. This, of course, does not mean that treating social anxiety would necessarily result in less susceptibility to infectious disease—a conclusion the authors do not reach—but the results were nevertheless startling. The authors suggest that there may be adjunctive psychiatric treatments appropriate for infectious diseases like HIV.

You might think some disorders would be pretty good justification for social anxiety. For example, people who stutter or those who have the severe trembling symptoms of Parkinson's disease might well be shy about showing those weaknesses in public—or at least you wouldn't be terribly surprised if they did demonstrate such reluctance. For these people, who can and do suffer ridicule from others, a bit of social anxiety might well be considered quite rational. And yet only about half of stutterers, for example, suffer from social anxiety. Why? What is protecting the other half? No one knows for sure, but the phenomenon certainly presents some interesting questions for researchers.

Other Social Problems

It isn't only psychiatric illnesses that can be predicted for people with social anxiety. Other problems accompany SAD as well. For example, girls with SAD are more likely to become pregnant as teenagers. This may instinctively seem a contradiction—after all, girls with social anxiety are less likely to have close romantic relationships, and, you would think, therefore less likely to become pregnant. But in fact socially anxious girls are more eager to be accepted and loved, and simultaneously less skilled at negotiating social or sexual situations. They are also less likely to use contraception or demand that their boyfriends use it.

Social anxiety affects educational attainment negatively as well. Interestingly, social phobia does not predict failure to graduate from high school or failure to finish college, but it does predict the failure to go from high school to college. This may be partly accounted for by the fear of socially anxious young people to leave home or encounter new social situations and challenges in making the transition from one school setting to another.

Prevention and Early Treatment

While it isn't 100 percent certain that treating SAD early will prevent other psychiatric problems from occurring, if the other problems associated with SAD can be prevented, SAD has to be treated before they occur. There is time to do this: typically, a person suffers with SAD for as long as ten years before serious mood disorders like depression set in. Treating SAD after depression or substance abuse has set in doesn't help in controlling other psychiatric illnesses. At that point, the other ailments must be treated as well. This means that treatment for SAD has to begin in the teenage years. Since kids don't come into treatment on their own, they have to be screened for this problem and then recruited into treatment. At least one project has done this successfully by going into schools and using self-administered anxiety and depression screening scales and then making efforts to reach out to affected students.

It is frustrating that one of the symptoms of social anxiety (and this is also true of some other psychiatric illnesses) is a reluctance to seek treatment. This means that people with social anxiety may fail to seek treatment not only for social anxiety itself but for other diseases. Social anxiety among people with eating disorders, for example, is common, and there is good evidence that having social anxiety interferes with seeking treatment for anorexia or bulimia, which can be life-threatening illnesses.

When SAD is not treated, it is an unremitting illness, with life-long negative consequences. It can last as long as thirty years, which is radically different from the much shorter course of a psychiatric illness like panic disorder. People with social anxiety disorder are significantly more likely to be unemployed, less likely to be married, and less likely to attain a high educational level than healthy people. Whether these facts are connected to social anxiety or to its comorbid illnesses is sometimes difficult to determine, but it is clear that the reason people with SAD go to doctors is often because of the comorbid illnesses and not the SAD itself. In fact, only about 5 percent of people with SAD alone seek mental health consultation.

Are You Sure It's Social Anxiety?

A kind of parlor game is making the rounds now—you can find it in various places around the Internet, and some versions circulate in e-mails—in which the reader is presented with words printed on a page and asked to name the color of the ink each word is printed in. The trick is that the words printed on the page are all names of colors, and the color of the ink in each case is different from the name of the color. Thus the reader sees the word *yellow* written in red ink. The correct response is "red," but most people hesitate, or even say "yellow," because the appearance of the type (red in color) is interfered with by its semantic content (the written word *yellow*). This phenomenon was first observed in the 1930s and is known as the Stroop effect, named for its discoverer. Researchers soon found that the hesitancy to say the correct word extended to other words closely associated with colors. For example, the same kinds of hesitancy and mistakes occur when a subject is presented with the word *grass* written in red ink, and asked to say the color of the ink often the subject will say, or start to say, "green."

Researchers quickly began to examine what happens when, instead of emotionally neutral words like colors, they presented people with emotionally charged words, asking them again simply to name the color of the ink. Would the emotional content of the words interfere with the task just as the semantic content did? The answer is yes—people reveal what kinds of words have strong emotional content by their hesitancies and mistakes in accomplishing this straightforward task.

By now you can probably see where I'm going with this. It didn't take long for scientists to begin using the test on people with psychiatric diagnoses. It has been used to study people with depression, phobias, post-traumatic stress disorder, and other diseases, and the results are consistent. For example, if you present words like *hairy* and *stinger* in brown type to people who are phobic about spiders, they're much slower to say "brown" than people who aren't afraid of those creatures. When you play this game with socially anxious people, they show a delayed response when the test uses words with social relevance that they don't show with neutral words. For example, if you present the word *blush,* their reaction in naming the color of the ink is slower than if you present a neutral word like *solid,* or a positive word like *baby.* Moreover, the effect begins to disappear as socially anxious people undergo treatment. In one study, treatment responders—including those who got better with cognitive behavioral treatment, administration of phenelzine (Nardil, an MAO inhibitor), and even those who responded to a placebo—did better on the test than nonresponders.

Private Feelings and Public Behavior

The test, simple as it is, is sensitive enough to distinguish between people with generalized anxiety disorder and those with social anxiety disorder. One study tested a group of patients with SAD (mostly people afraid of public speaking) against another group with generalized anxiety disorder. The SAD subjects reacted only to words related specifically to SAD (e.g., stutter, blush, embarrassment, audience) while the generalized anxiety patients reacted to these and others that didn't trouble the people with SAD (e.g., illness, injury, debts, abandoned). The test included neutral words as well, to which both groups reacted similarly.

My point is that people with social anxiety disorder have an inner life different from that of other people, different in specific and sometimes discernible ways. What appears perfectly benign to others elicits fear and anxiety in SAD sufferers. Yet at the same time, the observed behavior can be produced by very different inner states of mind. What is going on inside the brain of a person who "likes to be alone" is not a simple matter, and the diagnosis of SAD doesn't always account for it.

Suppose a person who shows all these symptoms of SAD just isn't interested in other people, simply doesn't want to interact with them. Is he still suffering from a psychiatric illness? Or does he have SAD only if it troubles him not to interact with others? What of people who are wary of others not because of SAD but because they have some other psychiatric diagnosis—avoidant personality disorder, for example. What of the inner life of a man who is suspicious of others because he has a psychotic illness like schizophrenia? What about people who have autism and are therefore unable to interact in normal social ways? How is their inner life different from that of someone with SAD? In short, what does it mean to be social, or not social?

Like many other animals, humans are naturally social beings. This can be shown physiologically: we process social information in circuits in the brain different from the ones that process other kinds of information. It can also be seen, for example, in the highly efficient way we process information about faces—usually, the most significant initial social interaction we have with other people. Our ability to do this is so refined that we can easily and accurately identify an almost unlimited number of people simply by looking them in the face. Moreover, most people can identify the emotions, intentions, and level of interest conveyed by different facial expressions with a high degree of accuracy, all of which is a great help if not an absolute necessity in facilitating verbal communication and comfortable social interaction. A few people know at a glance how to distinguish one bird species from another; others can tell at a glance the make and year of an automobile; but almost all of us are seasoned experts at distinguishing one face from all the thousands of others we've ever seen.

This ability to recognize faces and facial expression is centered in a specific part of the brain called the fusiform gyrus, but various parts of the brain probably participate in the process in what brain researchers call a distributed neural network. From MRI studies (see "Conclusion") of animals and of people with damaged brains, it is evident that the recognition of identity (who is it?) can be anatomically separate from the recognition of facial expression (how does he feel?). A person with brain defects in one of these separate areas can be perfectly capable of identifying a familiar face, but at the same time have no idea what the expression on that face is meant to convey. As you can imagine, the inability to distinguish a happy, angry, or puzzled expression on another's face can lead to considerable social uncertainty.

Even the way we interpret eye gaze is part of the way we function as social beings. Babies as young as six months can follow your eyes, trying to see what you are looking at. Why did this kind of "shared attention" ability evolve in primates, including humans? There is good reason to believe that it is designed not only to make others in the group aware of dangers from predators, but also to cement social relationships and facilitate communication in complex social groups.

Again, the inability to follow eye gaze can have a detrimental effect on social interaction and attachment.

Brain imaging has revealed other subtle aspects of social interaction. For example, most people can judge from facial expressions the emotions another person is feeling. But which part of the brain is involved in that perception depends on what emotion is being perceived. For example, in MRI studies, when a person is presented with a frightened or angry face, the amygdala goes into action, and people with lesions in this part of the brain have great difficulty in perceiving these emotions on a face presented to them. The perception of disgust, on the other hand, makes a different part of the brain "light up," the anterior insula, an area that is probably involved in processing smells and other visceral sensations.

From a very early age, infants prefer looking at faces to looking at other objects, and they quickly demonstrate an ability to mimic facial expressions. This suggests that the perception of faces and the understanding of facial expression is an integral part of developing social connections. Imagine an otherwise normal person whose amygdala prevents her from distinguishing a happy face from an angry one. Could such brain anatomy be the cause of some of the symptoms of social anxiety disorder? We are a long way from answering such questions.

Other Disorders

These experiments and investigations, fascinating and informative as they are, say little about the internal state of mind of people with problems in interacting socially. Determining someone's internal state of mind requires meeting with them face-to-face and talking with them at length and in ways quite different from ordinary social intercourse. After years of practice, I think I've gained at least some understanding of how to do this. People may reveal by means of a Stroop test or an MRI examination that they are in some way unusual, or deficient, in their ability to interact socially, but the disorder causing the problem is not revealed by any of these tests. And the cause of social functioning problems is not always social anxiety disorder. Most serious psychiatric illnesses involve some dysfunction in the area of relating to other people, but most serious psychiatric illnesses, even those whose primary feature is a problem in social interaction, are not SAD. It is those illnesses I want to discuss here.

AUTISM

As I suggested above, we're born to be social. Infants very early develop a fondness for looking at faces, smiling, cuddling and touching other people, laughing, playing socially interactive games like peek-a-boo, and so on. But some infants never seem to catch on to these normal activities. They are isolated, absorbed in their own world of peculiar routines and repetitive motions, uninterested in social interaction, especially with their peers. They demonstrate this tendency from infancy, and it persists as they grow. These children suffer from a pervasive developmental disorder called autism.

Autism usually becomes evident by the time a child is about three years old, when parents notice that he (it is usually a he—four times as many boys as girls have autism) doesn't want to play with other kids, or resists being touched or cuddled. Some cannot even make eye contact in the ways people normally do. They develop obsessive motions like rocking back and forth, or obsessively ordering their possessions and routines. Some demonstrate special abilities in specific areas like art or music. Their language is peculiar; they often refer to themselves in the third person, or simply echo the words others speak to them. When these symptoms are severe, few doctors—and few laypeople, for that matter—would confuse them with excessive shyness. But the symptoms can be mild, too, and under such circumstances, a child may just seem extremely bashful, may seem to be suffering from social anxiety disorder. But he is not, and the treatments for the two disorders are quite different, so making the distinction is essential. No one knows what causes autism, and its treatment is difficult and usually only partially successful. There is no cure. A child suspected of being autistic requires a comprehensive evaluation by a child psychiatrist or other autism expert, and a carefully designed program of behavioral and medical interventions.

ASPERGER'S DISORDER

This is another disorder, similar to autism in some ways but nevertheless a separately defined diagnosis, whose central feature is an inability to relate socially to other people, but which has nothing to do with social anxiety disorder. The symptoms of Asperger's disorder sometimes look a little like those of autism—the child seems socially eccentric, develops language early enough but often uses odd speech patterns, and has extreme difficulty in any social interactions with peers or adults. The Asperger's child usually has normal or even advanced language skills and functions at an intellectually higher level than a child with autism, but his intellectual interests are often peculiar or obsessive. He may want to spend hours a day watching trains go by as he counts the number of cars; he may be obsessed with meteorology, demanding to watch the Weather Channel all day long. Even such mundane things as subway stations or garbage trucks can become a preoccupation, and despite his intense interest and considerable knowledge of such things, he is uninterested in discussing the topic or sharing information with others. Often, Asperger's sufferers are physically clumsy, inflexible in their devotion to apparently meaningless routine, and friendless. Here again, though, SAD is not the problem. The treatment of Asperger's, like that of autism, requires a thorough evaluation and a program of psychotherapy, behavioral therapy, special education, medication, and support tailored to the individual child. Even though these children suffer from an inability to engage in normal social interaction, they do not suffer from social anxiety disorder.

SEPARATION ANXIETY DISORDER

Many infants go through a few months of separation anxiety around the age of eighteen months. They cling to their parents, are fearful of strangers, refuse to be held or touched by anyone except those familiar to them. This is considered a stage of normal development, and the anxiety passes with time and without any psychological or medical intervention. But separation anxiety can also occur in older children, usually around ages five to seven or eleven to fourteen. This kind of anxiety often first manifests itself in a refusal to go to school. Often the children become "ill" with minor complaints like stomachaches, headaches, or sore throats, symptoms that disappear if they are allowed to stay home. Their anxiety manifests itself in other ways as well. They feel unsafe except at home; they cling to their parents in ways inappropriate to their age; they demonstrate unrealistic fears of wild animals, intruders, monsters, or the dark. Sometimes, the anxiety can be so severe that they simply refuse to leave the house, or throw temper tantrums when forced to. Interestingly, it is the fear of leaving home that is the most prominent—when they get to school, they often calm down and function normally. Often the child knows his behavior is inappropriate to his age, and his embarrassment at his own fears can cause further anxiety, affecting his relationships with his peers. But this kind of "school anxiety" is not based on fears of socially interacting with other kids, and confusing it with social anxiety disorder would be a mistake. Treatment usually involves psychotherapy and medication, with the goal of returning the child to school as soon as possible.

REACTIVE ATTACHMENT DISORDER

The abnormal social relationships of this fairly uncommon disorder start early in life, usually in the first five years. It can manifest itself either as excessive sociability or its opposite. Some kids with this problem are happy to attach themselves to anyone, indiscriminately. Others are frozen with fear and resistant to any attempts to comfort them, unwilling to interact socially with anyone. The cause of this is severely inadequate care—children with inexperienced or disabled parents, children who have spent time in inadequate orphanages or other foster care, even children who because of physical illness have spent inordinate amounts of time hospitalized in psychologically inadequate conditions. Often these children have physical symptoms of inadequate care—growth delay, malnutrition, and so on. The inappropriate behavior of the child in cases such as this obviously has nothing whatever to do with social anxiety disorder, even though the failure to initiate or maintain social relationships is a central issue for them. Treatment for this disorder involves parental education, psychiatric treatment, and, in its most severe forms, separation of the child from the parents and hospitalization to provide suitable social environment, medical treatment, and psychiatric care. This is a massive intervention involving a multidisciplinary team of medical and psychiatric specialists, plus experts in social services and legal procedures.

DELUSIONAL DISORDER

Anxiety about interacting with other people comes in many guises. People suffering from delusional disorder can have a single, fixed, and totally erroneous idea. These are not the bizarre delusions of schizophrenia but delusions that are more or less plausible: being deceived by a lover, being followed or poisoned by someone, having a special relationship to a famous person, or suffering from an undiagnosed disease. The delusion exists by itself—functioning is normal except for whatever apparently irrational behavior the delusion induces. Sometimes the delusion can take a form that alters or prevents normal social intercourse: for example, a person with a delusional disorder may imagine she has a contagious disease that compels her to avoid social interactions for fear of infecting others. It is not social anxiety disorder that is preventing her from engaging other people; it is a specific delusion about a nonexistent problem. Treatment of delusional disorder usually involves both psychotherapy and medication, but since most delusional patients don't think there's anything wrong with them, it can be difficult to engage them in therapy. The disorder is relatively rare, and its treatment, which has not been scientifically evaluated, is based mostly on anecdotal evidence and clinical experience.

BODY DYSMORPHIC DISORDER

The *DSM-IV* categorizes this as a somatic disorder, but it bears some relationship to problems like obsessive-compulsive disorder, and the behavior it causes can look something like that associated with social anxiety disorder. In this disorder, a person becomes obsessed with a particular body part—nose, eyes, lips—convinced against all evidence that it is hideously ugly, bound to be ridiculed by others, and must at all costs be altered or concealed. Obviously, such an obsession or delusion can cause considerable reluctance to engage in normal social interactions, but this person is not suffering from social anxiety disorder. Treatment with cognitive behavioral therapy or SSRIs is effective. Some have recommended plastic surgery as a treatment, but there is no evidence that it really helps.

PERSONALITY DISORDERS

Certain personality disorders whose central features include an inability to engage in normal social intercourse should not be confused with social anxiety disorder. In fact, anxiety is not a feature of the disease at all. People with schizoid personality disorder—the disease usually has its onset in early adulthood—are almost completely divorced from interaction with others. They enjoy no close relationships, not even with family members, and they prefer to be alone. Sexual relationships don't interest them, they take little or no pleasure in normally pleasant activities, and they seem permanently cold and detached. Neither praise nor criticism seems to affect them one way or the other. This disorder should also not be confused with schizophrenia, a psychotic illness that causes hallucinations and delusions, although it can be a precursor to it.

Avoidant personality disorder also has its onset in early adulthood, and it is another disease whose symptoms overlap considerably with social anxiety. While a person with social anxiety can still enjoy intimate relationships, people with avoidant personality disorder show extreme restraint in all social relationships, even intimate ones, for fear of being criticized or disliked. They view themselves as inferior, inept, clumsy, and unappealing to other people. New activities of any kind terrify them—they are sure that any new undertaking will result in embarrassment or humiliation. If they get close to anyone, they are convinced that the person will discover "the real me," and be repulsed by what he finds. They feel they should avoid drawing attention to themselves because any attention will result in criticism, and the criticism will be both severe and completely justified. This sense of inferiority is one of the things that distinguishes avoidant personality disorder from SAD.

Personality disorders are notoriously difficult to treat. People who suffer from one usually don't recognize that there is anything wrong with them or believe there is anything worth changing. Although researchers have begun to explore medication for personality disorders, psychological interventions, especially cognitive behavioral therapy, are usually the treatments of choice.

Mild to Severe Spectrum

Further complicating the diagnostic picture is that the degree of ill-ness in social anxiety disorder spans a spectrum of mild to severe. The difference between someone who is just shy and someone who can benefit from treatment for social anxiety can be subtle. I want to emphasize that this complexity is one faced by patients and doctors in many other diseases, both medical and psychiatric. For example, if a person has a blood sugar of 120 mg/dl, he meets the definition for diabetes. But if someone has a blood sugar reading of 119, does that mean he's not diabetic and therefore not in need of treatment? Just as you can be slightly or more severely diabetic, you can be slightly or more severely socially anxious. Some researchers see a spectrum that runs from "shyness," which describes the low end of the range, to "social phobia" describing the middle range, to "avoidant personality disorder," at the extreme end.

In psychiatric diagnosis the internal state of mind of a complex human being cannot easily be discerned by simply observing his behavior. No one should imagine that all extreme shyness is social anxiety disorder. In fact, most extreme shyness is not that at all. Social anxiety disorder is a specific illness, and whether a person has it is not at all self-evident.

Children and Adolescents

Shy kids are easy to ignore. They don't bother anyone or attract attention like the noisier kids do. Their problems, such as they are, don't seem dramatic like those of kids with conduct disorder, for example, who act out and cause trouble. They present no difficulties, at least not to their adult caretakers. Their symptoms don't seem especially pathological—after all, what's wrong with minding your own business? It's easy to overlook such symptoms, or to conclude that they aren't really symptoms at all. This is part of the reason that social anxiety in children is undertreated. But it is estimated that about 5 percent of children suffer from the disorder, which starts, on average, at about eleven years old and gets worse in adolescence when school and social activities with peers begin to dominate youngsters' lives.

Social anxiety disorder almost always begins in childhood or adolescence. Cases in which the disease sets in after age twenty-five are rare, and when it develops for the first time in someone that old, it is usually in the context of another psychiatric illness, such as depression.

There is nothing new about the idea that children can be shy, but it is only recently that researchers have begun to understand that extreme social anxiety in children has severe negative effects that can last a lifetime. That shyness "runs in families" is an observation familiar since the very beginnings of the study of psychology, and there is little doubt that there is an inherited propensity to be shy (or not so shy). Studies of twins have borne this out—shyness exists in both identical twins about twice as often as it exists in fraternal twins. In fact, some studies have concluded that shyness is actually more heritable than other personality traits. Shyness in infants and young children can be demonstrated physiologically as well: shy babies presented with novel situations respond with higher heart rates, dilation of the pupils, and increased muscle tension compared to their less shy peers.

In younger kids, social anxiety sometimes leads to extreme guardedness, crying, or clinging to a parent or babysitter. By the time they are adolescents, kids developing social anxiety are almost constantly afraid of embarrassment or humiliation. Any exposure to a social situation, sometimes even the contemplation of such exposure, leads to feelings of panic. They stutter, fail to make eye contact, bite their nails, tremble in body or voice; sometimes they report that they are unable to organize their thoughts or stay focused. They are clearly in pain. When they refuse to perform a social task, or try to avoid it, they may be viewed by adults as defiant. "Terrified" would be a more apt one-word description.

What part of the problem is due to heredity and what part to the relationship kids have with their parents is hard to say, even though it has been widely studied. There are studies that appear to demonstrate that heredity is the overwhelmingly important factor in the development of social anxiety, and there are studies that conclude that parents' attitudes or personalities determine the fate of their kids in this domain. In any case, I will tell you what we know and help you decide what the studies mean to you.

the child's own personality or temperament. What parent would repeatedly force a terribly shy child into social situations that clearly make her uncomfortable? Parents of siblings often treat them in different ways, depending on the personality traits, abilities, likes, and dislikes of each child. It seems unexceptionable that parents would treat a child who likes playing soccer, for example, differently from one who prefers to spend his free time playing video games. Why wouldn't they? Parents' behavior surely affects that of their children, but let's not forget that the behavior of children can also affect that of their parents.

Blaming parents—or inspiring parents to blame themselves—is unfair and unproductive. First, what our children inherit genetically can in no reasonable way be considered our "fault." Second, any parent of a socially anxious child who has taken the trouble to pick up this book is obviously trying to do the best for his child. So let's dispense with blaming the parents and get on with the job of helping our children, whatever their issues and problems, to grow into successful and happy adults.

Predicting the Development of Social Anxiety

How can you tell which kids are going to develop social anxiety later in childhood or early adolescence? A recent Harvard Medical School study found that highly inhibited two-year-olds were about twice as likely as their less-inhibited peers to develop social anxiety as teenagers. This connection didn't hold for specific phobia, separation anxiety, or performance anxiety—only for social anxiety. An even larger Australian study had much the same results—shy kids are more likely to develop into adolescents with social anxiety disorder. Interestingly, most shy kids didn't develop into socially anxious teenagers, and most socially anxious teenagers were not especially shy when they were little. So there was some predictive value to being shy as a little kid, but it was limited.

With all the problems kids face and parents have to help them deal with, excessive shyness may seem a rather minor matter. And for most kids, it probably is. A certain amount of shyness is normal, and even a kind of excessive shyness at various times in a child's life is to be expected. Between the ages of six months and fifteen months, for example, children often experience a period of "stranger anxiety," a phenomenon familiar to most parents. In fact, total lack of stranger anxiety could point to other developmental problems such as autism or Asperger's disorder. Most shyness in older kids, and even adolescents, can be overcome with the passage of time and some gentle help from understanding parents. That's why a doctor doesn't make a diagnosis of social anxiety in a child until certain specific criteria have been met. For one thing, the anxiety has to be persistent— it has to last more than six months. The age of the child has to be considered as well. We are looking for behavior that is inappropriate to the child's age, not ordinary development that includes periods of shyness or awkwardness. In a child, the pathological shyness of social anxiety is not contained or hidden the way it can be in adults—kids with social anxiety act troubled in easily observable ways. Unlike adult sufferers, socially anxious children faced with a social situation cry, have tantrums, hide, visibly panic, or verbally refuse to interact. Finally, a kid who's shy only with adults but not with other children would not be considered to have social anxiety.

Even though infants can have stranger anxiety, they can't suffer from social anxiety because the disorder depends on being able to experience shame, guilt, or the disapproval of other people. Children as young as four or five begin to realize that others can have different opinions from their own, and they may start to experience shame, but the real problems of social anxiety usually don't begin until just before adolescence. By age ten or so, children begin to be responsible for acting on their own, in school, in recreational activities, in forming friendships without the intervention of their parents, and it is at this point that self-awareness blooms. More than half of all kids experience some kind of severe anxiety about some social task during adolescence, but only a minority suffer the extreme symptoms of social anxiety disorder.

I try to gently motivate socially anxious kids, give them praise for small steps toward social interaction. My general approach is to tell them to go toward the fear rather than avoid it. I urge them—and I urge parents to join me in this—to prove to themselves that they can master the fear. This is very important because kids can get into a pattern of avoiding things, and this can develop into avoidant personality disorder. What we don't want to do is get into a battle about it. Gently motivate, and give praise. The idea is that once they automatically go toward the fear rather than avoid it, they have really overcome the problem. Many people start out being shy kids, but when they can automatically face what they fear, they grow into socially adept adults.

Severe social anxiety can interfere with normal development, prevent a child from making friends, destroy pleasure in school activities, affect academic work, and make a kid completely miserable. Moreover, it can have lifelong negative effects. Parents have a responsibility to do something about this, of course, but blaming them for their children's social anxiety is at best a waste of time. Even if they are in any way at fault—and the evidence that they are is weak and often contradictory—so what? You still have to deal with the problem, and assigning blame for it won't make it go away. The disorder spontaneously disappears in only a minority of cases, and most adults with social anxiety have had it since they were teenagers. When the problem your child is having is severe, you won't be able to solve it yourself, and no reasonable person could expect you to. Seeking professional help, backed by your own knowledge of the facts, is essential.

I do not want to suggest that families and family dynamics have absolutely nothing to do with social anxiety in children; I only want to avoid finger-pointing. In chapter 8, we'll discuss some of the ways in which families, and family therapy, can have a positive role in helping kids with social anxiety.

Temperament

All parents notice that their infants have a certain temperament that seems to exist even from the earliest months of their lives. Sometimes they notice it more with a second child, who seems so different in his moods and preferences from the first. Infants seem to have more or less built-in and unchangeable temperamental or personality traits demonstrated at an age so young that no outside influence could have produced them, traits that persist as the child grows. Sometimes shyness is among them.

With a problem like social anxiety disorder, distinguishing personality traits from psychiatric symptoms is often problematic, and even the most experienced psychiatrists can have difficulty in deciding which is which. That some personality traits can be a precursor to social anxiety disorder makes the problem even more difficult. A 1988 study tried to figure out whether what the researchers call "behavioral inhibition," a trait found in about 10 to 15 percent of white American children, can be a sign that social anxiety will develop. Behavioral inhibition is similar to extreme shyness, but differs in that it applies to all kinds of novel situations, not just social ones. Young children with this problem demonstrate reticence, fear, avoidance, or sometimes just quiet restraint when faced with any new situation or object, or an unfamiliar person, whether an adult or another child. When the researchers looked at the physiological reactions these kids had when exposed to novel situations, they found they were similar to those of older children with test anxiety and adults with social anxiety disorder. They also discovered that this kind of behavior, found as early as infancy, persists through older childhood and adolescence, and that when these kids become teenagers, they are much more likely to suffer from generalized social anxiety than their less inhibited peers. There is also evidence that this trait is heritable: behaviorally inhibited children have parents with higher rates of social anxiety than the parents of noninhibited kids. The personality trait, in other words, can exist at one end of a behavioral spectrum of which psychiatric illness is the other end, and the personality trait can sometimes be a precursor of the illness.

Social Anxiety from the Child's Point of View

The effects of social anxiety on the emotional and social lives of children and adolescents have not been widely studied, but nevertheless some useful findings exist. It is particularly interesting that children ranked by their teachers as highly anxious are consistently less well liked by their peers than their non-anxious classmates. In other words, other children don't get along well with kids who are socially anxious. The failure to make friends in childhood is not a good sign for successful adult social adjustment.

Sadly, kids with social anxiety usually don't like themselves very much, either. They lack self-esteem, see themselves as outsiders, incompetent compared to their less anxious peers. They are overly self-conscious, excessively concerned with how others view them; they withdraw, they avoid social contact, and of course they lack friends. Even activities they want to participate in are beyond their reach because they can't face the social interactions that many activities involve. Children with social anxiety report more nervousness about meeting new people, more negative interactions with peers, more instances of being teased, and more enemies among their schoolmates. You might intuitively believe that kids who are isolated or inhibited and repeatedly rejected by peers would become even more isolated and inhibited, and you're right. The negative responses they provoke in other kids often serve to confirm their worst suspicions about themselves. Once the pattern of avoiding social contact is established and the opportunity for social interaction restricted, these kids get less practice in using social skills, and what social skills they have begin to deteriorate, reinforcing their belief in their own inferiority. The child's belief that "they don't like me" or that "they're mean" is reinforced by the child's own reluctance to engage in social interactions. There is a vicious circle of social anxiety, rejection, and depression leading to more social anxiety.

Avoiding school is one of the most troubling consequences. When these kids say they don't feel like going to school today, they're panicked and really can't go. Kids who don't attend school regularly miss out on essential social and developmental opportunities, not to mention the disastrous effects on intellectual progress and academic performance. School avoidance is very hard to treat, and even with the best care, with inpatient hospitalization, about half of these school-avoidant kids continue to demonstrate significant school avoidance.

As socially anxious children reach adolescence, they begin having other troubles. They don't date, they don't participate in sports, they don't speak up in class, they avoid oral class presentations. Some become the class "nerds," the objects of pity or ridicule, the victims of bullies, the eternal outsiders. Teenagers with social anxiety have few friends and their academic work suffers. Needless to say, none of this improves their self-esteem or self-confidence and only serves to increase anxiety further. In a study of adolescents, the shyest boys were more likely to use drugs and alcohol than those who were less shy, but this wasn't true of the girls—suggesting that shyness is more of a problem for boys than girls.

Social anxiety is, for many kids, a constant misery, with both psychological and physical symptoms. Just thinking about a social interaction, even hours or days before it is to happen, can provoke unpleasant feelings and painful physical symptoms including rapid heartbeat, sweating, and feelings of panic.

In children and adolescents, it's much more common to see social anxiety along with other psychiatric problems than to see it in its "pure" form. Many studies have consistently concluded that social anxiety in children and adolescents is often accompanied by other anxiety disorders and by mood disorders like major depression. In one study, fewer than one-third of the kids with social phobia had no other psychiatric problem, and one-fifth of them had three or more diagnoses. This kind of pattern is seen in other studies as well—about two-thirds of kids with social anxiety suffer from some other psychiatric problem at the same time. Generalized anxiety disorder, attention deficit hyperactivity disorder, and specific phobias are also common. Although it hasn't been specifically shown in adolescents, social anxiety in adults is associated with higher rates of attempted suicide.

The effects of social anxiety in the teenage years persist into adulthood because the disorder interferes with normal development. It is associated with the failure to complete high school in girls and the failure to enter or complete college in both males and females. To the extent that educational success is essential to success in career achievement and developing financial security, kids with social anxiety will suffer in these areas as well. Children with social anxiety are at risk for long-term problems in many domains: social relationships, romantic attachments, workplace success, family life. Add depression and substance abuse, for which kids with social anxiety are also at risk, and you have a recipe for disaster. Treating social anxiety early is essential to avoiding these long-term adverse outcomes.

Selective Mutism

The absolute refusal to speak in front of unfamiliar people is one of the most severe symptoms of social anxiety disorder in children, and, although this is a rare phenomenon (it occurs in less than 1 percent of the population, and more frequently in girls than in boys), it can be one of the earliest to appear. It was once thought that this selective mutism was not connected to social anxiety, but we now believe that it can be one of the precursors of adult SAD.

The most prominent symptom of the illness is an inability to speak in at least one situation, usually in the classroom, despite perfectly fluent speech in other situations. This used to be called "elective" mutism, implying that it was a choice on the part of the child, but the *DSM-IV* now uses the term "selective," which suggests an involuntary nature in a refusal to speak, reflecting current beliefs that mutism has its origins in anxiety. It must be remembered that most speech difficulties in children are not due to this rather uncommon disorder, and arriving at a diagnosis of selective mutism requires the physician to eliminate every other possible cause for a speech problem.

Earlier theories about the origins of selective mutism tended to round up the usual suspects: overbearing mothers and distant fathers, sexual abuse or other trauma, unresolved psychodynamic conflicts, divorce, death of a loved one, even frequent moving from one house to another. But there is no study that establishes such causes, and all these explanations now seem unsatisfactory. The resemblance between selectively mute children and socially anxious adults is now believed to be much more significant. The disorder almost certainly has a genetic component, and first-degree relatives of kids with selective mutism suffer from anxiety disorders in greater numbers than the rest of the population.

Parents often report that "she's always been this way," suggesting that the onset of the mutism disorder is early and gradual. It usually doesn't become evident until the child reaches school age and has to speak in more or less public situations without familiar caretakers present. A large majority of kids with selective mutism also meet the criteria for social anxiety, and they also commonly suffer from other psychiatric problems, especially other anxiety disorders and phobias.

Treating these kids means overcoming one giant (and obvious) hurdle: they won't talk to you. The place to begin is with the parents, getting a thorough description of the symptoms and the history of the problem. Here is where the doctor has to sort out the many other problems that cause speech difficulties to make sure that selective mutism is really the problem. Physical problems might underlie the mutism, and these have to be sought out. Since there are always genetic components to consider, I'll want to know about any family history of shyness or anxiety.

The child should always have a thorough physical and neurological examination, including a hearing test. Looking for the common and obvious is essential before leaping to conclusions about a disorder as unusual as selective mutism. Psychological testing for cognitive ability is also essential, especially since these children sometimes can't be assessed accurately by conventional academic standards. I'll want to know if there are any learning disabilities or deficits in intellectual capacity. If the parents have, or can make, a tape of the child speaking at home, I would want to listen to it.

Once all that is done, I want to communicate with the child, even if she doesn't want to talk. With some kids, drawing or playing games is a way to get through, and even if the child won't speak, she may communicate by nodding or smiling or giggling.

Various techniques have been tried for treating selective mutism, and although none have been scientifically and systematically studied, there are approaches that seem to work. Behavioral techniques that offer reinforcement for speaking and no reinforcement for failure to speak take some time to show their effects, but they do work in many cases. Psychodynamic (talk therapy) and family therapy have fallen out of favor for this disorder; the former takes too long and depends too much on speech, the latter has virtually disappeared because there is little evidence that family pathology is a cause of the problem. Pharmacotherapy has been tried, with phenelzine (Nardil, an MAO inhibitor) and the selective serotonin uptake inhibitors fluvoxamine (Luvox) and fluoxetine (Prozac). Speech therapy sometimes helps. None of these techniques works for all children, and each has its defects.

Treating Adolescents for Social Anxiety

I discuss at some length the treatment of social anxiety with psychological therapy in chapter 9 and with pharmacological treatments in chapter 10. The psychological, that is, the cognitive behavioral treatment of adolescents is in most respects not radically different from that of adults. But there is at least one important distinction: with adolescents, the participation of parents is important. Parents have to function as teachers or coaches between sessions and after the therapy concludes.

As in adult treatment, the program is a brief group therapy with other socially anxious youngsters, usually about twelve to fifteen sessions. The therapy involves skills training, structured practice in simulated social situations, repeated exposure in the real world to anxiety-provoking interactions, and homework assignments with careful recordkeeping. The exact contribution of each of these components is difficult to estimate, but there is no question about the effectiveness of the whole program, both immediately after therapy and in the long term.

Although teenagers are sometimes treated with medicines for social anxiety, it would be rare for a youngster to take medicine alone with no psychotherapy. In chapter 10 we'll discuss the complex problems and some current controversies concerning psychiatric medicines for teenagers.

❖ AN UNUSUAL CASE OF AN UNUSUAL DISORDER

I once treated an unusual case: two adult male siblings, a little more than one year apart in age, with identical symptoms of selective mutism. They're college students, though not at the same college. They decided to "split up" when they graduated from high school not because they didn't get along (they were and are best of friends), but because each of them thought it would be a good idea to get out on his own for a while. When they speak, it's almost impossible to hear them. They have difficulty entering a room, they wear their hair over their faces to hide their eyes, they speak quietly, they exit the room backward to avoid turning their backs to you. But the brothers are quite bright and highly motivated, willing to put themselves in positions where they have quite a lot of performance stress—they don't try to avoid it. Both are good students and have achieved some real success through a combination of appropriate medications and behavioral approaches. In fact, one plans to become a school psychologist, a position that demands on occasion a degree of assertiveness of which he is probably not yet capable. Yet they are able to interact with others, go to college, and set and attain goals. Fortunately, they have a very supportive family, which of course is essential in such cases.

What's a Parent to Do?

Can parents force kids into treatment who don't want to go? With preadolescents maybe. With adolescents, almost certainly not. Adolescents have to be persuaded that treatment is necessary and that it will do them some good, and it is not always easy for even the most well-intentioned parents to accomplish this. There is no point whatever in bringing in an uncooperative teenager for treatment that requires his total cooperation. At home, a parent can help in getting the teenager and the family to recognize that social anxiety disorder is a medical problem, not a character flaw. I help parents and teenagers alike to understand that it isn't useful to beat themselves up for this—they're not the only ones facing this problem. I gently reinforce and praise a teenager for his social behavior, and convince the family to do that too. If a kid reports that he was able to enter the lunchroom today without panicking, that's an accomplishment that ought to be noticed—it isn't trivial: "That's great. Maybe next time you'll be able to sit at a table where other kids are already seated. But just getting in there without your heart beating fast is good work! Maybe you want to try it again tomorrow, and see how it feels." And when it doesn't go so well, no criticism is necessary—the kid is feeling bad enough already: "Well, just because you couldn't talk to those guys this time doesn't mean it won't work if you give it another shot. Wait a day or two, and maybe you'll want to try again. There's no rush anyway."

For teens, it's important to identify what the motivating factor for change is—the treatment can be emotionally painful and having a goal to achieve is important. It's important also to specify how the SAD is preventing them from getting something they want—a girlfriend or boyfriend, participation in team sports, strong career goals—and can't get because of the anxiety. Often participation in a drama club can be an easy opening for a kid with social anxiety. Such an activity allows him to hide behind a role, but at the same time get involved with other kids in the production of a play. Team sports may be helpful in similar ways. Maybe there are other after-school activities that a shy kid is interested in and can be encouraged to pursue, but these should be activities that involve as much social contact with other kids as possible.

I urge parents to form their own alliance with the teenager; the therapist is not the agent of the parents and shouldn't act as if he is. I need an independent alliance with the teen. I'm on his side, and I want him to understand this. It's helpful for the youngster to see that SAD is something to fight against—it's not who he is and it's not a flaw in his character. It's a roadblock in the way of doing what he really wants to do. I urge teens to take small steps, identify things they don't see as overwhelming but can have success with, and in the process attain some self-satisfaction and maybe even a little outside praise.

Treatment is not the only answer. Parents can certainly help kids with social anxiety. Indeed, even with treatment, the help of parents and other adults is essential. Often kids with social anxiety have parents with social anxiety. Such parents are extremely sensitive to the stress their kids are feeling, and they become overprotective, shielding them from social interactions that they should encourage their children to face. Instead of providing a means of avoiding the situation, parents should deemphasize the importance of it. What parents should not do is get into an emotional battle, forcing the kid to do something in some sort of punitive way. They should be giving positive feedback each time the kid faces a situation, encouraging him to try it again in even bolder ways. Parents can help their youngster get a more realistic idea of what others think of him—to avoid irrational thoughts about how "obvious" his supposed inadequacies are to everyone. The essential rule: never reward or encourage avoidant behavior. Parents should reward even small steps in facing social situations.

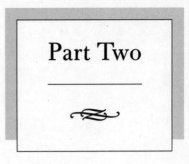

Part Two

On Your Own: Self-Tests for Shyness and Exercises to Help Overcome It

While self-tests, even the well-designed tests I'm going to describe here, are not a substitute for professional diagnosis, they can give you some idea of where you stand in relation to other people on the scale of social anxiety. Self-tests can be used as a tool to determine with some objectivity how much your difficulty in dealing with social situations is actually affecting the way you live, or getting in the way of how you want to live. Exercises to combat extreme shyness can also be done on your own, without a diagnosis of social anxiety and without formal psychotherapy. Not everyone suffering from extreme shyness needs professional help. Cognitive behavioral therapy, the most commonly used form of psychotherapy for social anxiety, depends a lot on doing homework on your own without the presence or help of a professional.

Self-Tests and Questionnaires

You may wonder why you would need a test to determine how shy you are. After all, you know what makes you shy, you know what kinds of public tasks you face with great trepidation, and you're perfectly aware of the ones you want to avoid completely. But sometimes this isn't enough. Sometimes the avoidance of a social interaction becomes so ingrained that seeing it as any kind of problem is difficult—you may not even be aware of how much it is getting in the way of accomplishing your goals and doing the things you want to do. Using self-tests like those described here can sometimes help.

Some tests or scales are designed to be used by clinicians and administered to patients. Adaptations of these same scales can be used as self-tests. I want to emphasize that these self-tests are not the same as the "test your personality" features that appear in popular magazines. Typically, these magazine articles are merely exercises in tautology: "Do you feel shy in front of people?" the test asks, and then offers three choices: Often, Sometimes, and Never. If you answer "Often" you get three points, two points for "Sometimes," and one for "Never." This sort of test tells you nothing about your actual social interactions or the psychology behind them—it merely confirms what you've said by assigning it a number. By contrast, the self-tests that follow have been carefully studied using complex statistical analyses to determine they are reliable and consistent from one person to another, and that they predict certain kinds of psychological phenomena accurately. Moreover, they have been widely used with thousands of subjects so that norms of social behavior can be established by looking at the results produced by many people with and without the diagnosis of social anxiety.

Many scales have been designed by psychologists, psychiatrists, and others to test for social anxiety disorder, and the selection here is from the most recently developed ones. In addition to scales and questionnaires devoted exclusively to social anxiety, a number of well-tested scales for phobias and other anxiety disorders include questions on social anxiety as well. I don't want to imply that you can diagnose yourself by using one of these scales, or any other scale you may find elsewhere. You can't. An experienced clinician is the only one who can arrive at the proper diagnosis. Your rating on these scales, however, could give you some idea of whether seeking treatment by an experienced clinician might be useful.

Social Phobia Inventory

This scale, first published in 2000, assesses fear, avoidance, and physiological symptoms, which makes it somewhat different from other self-rating scales in use. It is based on an interviewer-administered scale, the Brief Social Phobia Scale (see below) and its authors, researchers at Duke University, have broad goals for it: to distinguish between those with a diagnosis of social phobia and those without; to indicate severity of symptoms; to recognize symptoms as they vary over time; to distinguish those with and without social anxiety; and to distinguish the effects of various treatments on the course of the illness. The authors have also developed a brief version of this questionnaire called the Mini-SPIN, which has shown some usefulness as a tool in screening for social anxiety.

The test consists of 17 behaviors that the test taker is asked to evaluate on a 5-point scale: 0 = not at all, 1 = a little bit, 2 = somewhat, 3 = very much, 4 = extremely. Here are the 17 items:

1. I am afraid of people in authority.
2. I am bothered by blushing in front of people.
3. Parties and social events scare me.

4. I avoid talking to people I don't know.
5. Being criticized scares me a lot.
6. Fear of embarrassment causes me to avoid doing things or speaking to people.
7. Sweating in front of people causes me distress.
8. I avoid going to parties.
9. I avoid activities in which I am the center of attention.
10. Talking to strangers scares me.
11. I avoid having to give speeches.
12. I would do anything to avoid being criticized.
13. Heart palpitations bother me when I am around people.
14. I am afraid of doing things when people might be watching.
15. Being embarrassed or looking foolish are among my worst fears.
16. I avoid speaking to anyone in authority.
17. Trembling or shaking in front of others is distressing to me.

A score above 19 correlates highly with people diagnosed with social anxiety disorder—that is, people who have been clinically examined and diagnosed with social anxiety, tend to score above 19 on this test.*

The Liebowitz Social Anxiety Scale

This clinician-administered scale was developed by M. R. Liebowitz at Columbia University and the New York State Psychiatric Institute and first published in 1987. It lists 24 social situations and asks the patient to rate himself on a scale of 1 to 4, first on how much he fears a given situation and then how much he tries to avoid it. An electronic

---

*Adapted from K. M. Connor, J. R. Davidson, L. E. Churchill, et al. "Psychometric Properties of the Social Phobia Inventory (SPIN). New Self-Rating Scale." *British Journal of Psychiatry* 176 (April 2000): 379–86. Used by permission.

version fully equipped with drop-down boxes and automatic tallying of the score, can be found at h+ttp://www.anxietyhelp.org/information/leibowitz.html. (Yes, you have to misspell Dr. Liebowitz's name—otherwise you won't find it!) Here's what the test* looks like in the printed version:

Fear or Anxiety
0 = None
1 = Mild
2 = Moderate
3 = Severe

Avoidance
0 = Never (0%)
1 = Occasionally (1–33%)
2 = Often (33–67%)
3 = Usually (67–100%)

	Fear or Anxiety	*Avoidance*
1. Telephoning in public		
2. Participating in small groups		
3. Eating in public places		
4. Drinking with others in public places		
5. Talking to people in authority		
6. Acting, performing, or giving a talk in front of an audience		
7. Going to a party		
8. Working while being observed		
9. Writing while being observed		
10. Calling someone you don't know very well		

*Adapted from M. R. Liebowitz. *Social Phobia.* "Modern Problems in Psychopharmacology." 22 (1987): 141–73. Used by permission.

	Fear or Anxiety	Avoidance
11. Talking with people you don't know very well		
12. Meeting strangers		
13. Urinating in a public bathroom		
14. Entering a room when others are already seated		
15. Being the center of attention		
16. Speaking up at a meeting		
17. Taking a test		
18. Expressing a disagreement or disapproval to people you don't know very well		
19. Looking people you don't know very well in the eyes		
20. Giving a report to a group		
21. Trying to pick up someone		
22. Returning goods to a store		
23. Giving a party		
24. Resisting a high-pressure salesperson		

You can take the test, add up your numbers, and score yourself—no special expertise or training is required. Each item consists of a given situation, the rate of anxiety (0 to 3 = none, mild, moderate, severe) and the rate of avoidance (0 to 3 = never, occasionally, often, usually). Generally speaking, a score of 55 to 65 indicates moderate social phobia, 65 to 80 marked social phobia, 80 to 95 severe social phobia, and greater than 95 very severe social phobia. Here is the version of the LSAS adapted for children and adolescents.* There are 24 behaviors, and the same rating scale is used as for the adult version:

	Anxiety	Avoidance
1. Talking to teachers, other adults		
2. Standing up to talk in front of the class		
3. Speaking up/raising hand to speak		
4. Giving a report in class		
5. Calling someone unfamiliar on the telephone		
6. Trying to make friends or a date		
7. Talking with other unfamiliar children		
8. Expressing disagreement to someone not known well		
9. Answering the telephone		
10. Meeting strangers		
11. Being the center of attention		
12. Participating in small groups		
13. Resisting pressure to join in		
14. Looking people in the eyes		
15. Going to a party		
16. Taking a test		

*Adapted from E. S. Dummit III, R. G. Klein, N. K. Tancer, et al. "Systematic Assessment of 50 Children with Selective Mutism." *Journal of the American Academy of Child Adolescent Psychiatry* 36(5) (May 1997): 653–60. Used by permission.

	Anxiety	Avoidance
17. Returning something borrowed or bought		
18. Entering a room when others are seated		
19. Working in class while others are watching		
20. Writing in class while others are watching		
21. Urinating in a public restroom		
22. Having a party		
23. Eating in school or restaurants		
24. Drinking in school or restaurants		

The Social Thoughts and Beliefs Scale

This test centers around the thoughts of people with social anxiety disorder. Cognitive theory holds that social anxiety can be traced to irrational or erroneous thought processes. This scale helps you articulate those thoughts and reveal how strong they are. It consists of a list of common thoughts or beliefs and asks the patient to rate himself on how characteristic a given thought is on a 5-point scale as follows: Never, Rarely, Sometimes, Often, or Always. Here are the 21 statements* that make up the inventory:

1. When I am in a social situation, I appear clumsy to other people.

---

*Adapted from S. M. Turner, M. R. Johnson, D. C. Beidel, et al. "The Social Thoughts and Beliefs Scale: A New Inventory for Assessing Cognitions in Social Phobia." *Psychological Assessment* 15(3) (September 2003): 384–91. Used by permission.

2. If I am with a group of people and I have an opinion, I am likely to chicken out and not say what I think.
3. I feel as if other people sound more intelligent than I do.
4. When I am with other people, I am not good at standing up for myself.
5. I am a coward when it comes to interacting with other people.
6. I feel unattractive when I am with other people.
7. I would never be able to make a good speech in public.
8. Other people are more comfortable in social situations than I am.
9. Other people are more socially capable than I am.
10. No matter what I do, I will always be uncomfortable in social situations.
11. My mind is very likely to go blank when I am talking in a social situation.
12. I am not good at making small talk.
13. Other people are bored when they are around me.
14. When speaking in a group, others will think what I am saying is stupid.
15. If I am around someone I am interested in, I am likely to get panicky or do something to embarrass myself.
16. I do not know how to behave when I am in the company of others.
17. If something went wrong in a social situation, I would not be able to smooth it over.
18. When I am with other people, they usually don't think I am very smart.
19. When other people laugh, it feels as if they are laughing at me.
20. People can easily see when I am nervous.
21. If there is a pause during a conversation, I feel as if I have done something wrong.

The authors, from the departments of Psychiatry at Duke University and Menninger Phoenix, show that the scale accurately discriminates between people with social anxiety, people with other anxiety disorders, and those with no psychiatric disorder at all. Although you can't diagnose yourself with this test (or with any of the others described here) the mean score for people with SAD is 52, and for people who don't suffer from social anxiety, 22.

The Social Phobia and Anxiety Inventory for Children

The authors call this a "new inventory to assess childhood social anxiety and phobia," and it is designed for and tested with children 8 to 17 years old. Scores on the test successfully distinguish socially anxious and non-socially-anxious children. The child rates the statement for the extent of distress a given situation causes on a 3-point scale: 0 = never or hardly ever, 1 = sometimes, 2 = almost always or always. The scale* is divided into four different categories of behavior as follows:

Assertiveness
Asked to do something I don't want to do
Feel scared when ignored or made fun of
Something said that is wrong or bad
Somebody starts arguing with me
Feel scared in an embarrassing situation
Too scared to ask questions in class
Feel scared in a school day, choir, music, or dance recital

---

*Adapted from D. C. Beidel, S. M. Turner, and C. M. Fink. "Assessment of Childhood Social Phobia: Construct, Convergent, and Discriminative Validity of the Social Phobia and Anxiety Inventory for Children (SPAI-C)." *Psychological Assessment* 8 (1996): 235–40.

General Conversation
Feel scared to meet new kids
Feel scared when I start to talk to a new kid
Feel scared when speaking in front of the class
Feel scared when with others and I have to do something while
    they watch
Feel scared when joining a social situation with a large group
Feel scared if I have to talk longer than a few minutes

Physical and Cognitive Symptoms
In a social situation, I feel (physical symptoms)
Before a social situation, I feel (physical symptoms)
When with others, I think scary thoughts
Before going somewhere, I worry about what might go wrong

Avoidance
Avoid social situations
Leave social situations
Feel so scared I go home early
Feel scared when become the center of attention

Public Performance
Feel scared when speaking or reading in class
Feel scared when answering questions in class
Feel scared when speaking in front of a group
Feel scared when others watch me do something

A cutoff score of 18 discriminates fairly accurately between children who are socially anxious and those who are not.

The Brief Social Phobia Scale

This test* is a little different from the others, but I wanted to include it because it is one of the few that includes specific physiological reactions. This is an observer-rated scale—that is, it was designed and tested with the intention of having someone pose these questions to the patient, and it was researched by J. R. Davidson and others with groups of patients who intended to be treated for social anxiety. It includes three subscales: fear, avoidance, and physiological arousal symptoms. Its authors have demonstrated that it is a sensitive measure of social phobia. Fear and avoidance, the authors point out, are both included because some patients may fear certain situations, but not avoid them. This may be especially true of patients with discrete fears, such as public speaking. Here are the items the interviewer would ask a patient to rate on a 5-point scale, 1 being least feared or avoided:

How much do you fear:
Speaking in public
Talking to people in authority
Talking to strangers
Being embarrassed or humiliated
Being criticized
Social gatherings
Doing something while being watched

How much do you avoid:
Speaking in public

---

*Adapted from J. R. Davidson, C. M. Miner, J. De Veaugh-Geiss, et al. "The Brief Social Phobia Scale: A Psychometric Evaluation." *Psychological Medicine* 27(1) (January 1997): 161–66.

Talking to people in authority
Talking to strangers
Being embarrassed or humiliated
Being criticized
Social gatherings
Doing something while being watched

How much do you feel these symptoms in contemplating social interactions (1 to 5 scale, least to most):
Blushing
Palpitations
Tremor
Sweating

Socially anxious patients who undergo treatment score lower on this test after treatment than before, and the test is a fairly sensitive measure of treatment success. The mean total score on this test—remember, this was tested with people who had already been diagnosed with social phobia—was 42.

Setting Up an Exercise Program

Like any homework, exercises to combat social anxiety can be difficult, and there are always plenty of excuses for putting them off, doing them superficially, or not doing them at all. But don't neglect them: the results are worth the effort.

The first thing to do in setting up an exercise program for yourself—or in having your therapist help you set it up, as I often do—is to decide what you fear least, what you fear less, and what you fear most of all. If you've completed a few of the self-questionnaires above, you've probably got a pretty good idea where you stand. There may be many social situations that trouble you, but concentrating on one at a time is the best approach. For example, say you work in sales and are obliged from time to time to present sales presentations before large audiences at national sales conferences. You've avoided this for years, because your fear of public speaking is overwhelming. Yet public presentations are extremely important to your career success, so this fear is a primary symptom of social anxiety you need to eliminate. Of course, some kinds of speech are less anxiety provoking than others, and you might rank your fears this way:

1. Least anxiety provoking (causes no physical symptoms, but some slight anxiety): speaking to more than one colleague in an informal setting.
2. Somewhat anxiety provoking (causes some slight physical symptoms—e.g., increased heartbeat—and still presents considerable difficulty): speaking in a formal meeting to a small group of colleagues at work.
3. Most anxiety provoking (causes overwhelming physical symptoms—e.g., blushing, sweating, shaking, rapid heartbeat; almost impossible to overcome): presenting in front of a large group of colleagues at a national sales conference.

Your final goal is to be able to carry off a speech at a large conference, but it's important to set some intermediate goals first. For example:

1. Prepare a presentation at home, and perform it alone, imagining an audience.
2. Perform a presentation in front of a close friend or family member.
3. Do the same presentation in front of three or more friends and family members at once.

These are modest goals, far short of performing a full-length speech in front of a company-wide audience, but success with modest goals is the first step. There's no point in setting your first exercises at a level that will immediately defeat you. Once these goals are accomplished, you can set more stringent tasks for yourself, but there is no rush right now.

It's important to keep a written record of your progress (and even of your lack of progress), so you should develop a method of ranking your success at accomplishing each of these exercises. One good way—it's not the only way—is to assign yourself an anxiety score, 1 to 10, at the end of each practice session. A 1 indicates very mild anxiety that doesn't really interfere with your activity. A 10 indicates overwhelming, paralyzing fear. In between is the range of moderate to severe anxiety you might feel in the social situation. If you do this in writing each time, you can track your progress accurately, instead of depending on your memory. Adding notes on the physical or psychological symptoms you experienced with each exercise will provide further important detail. Did my heart beat fast when I performed the exercise? Was I dizzy? Did I start to feel faint? Did my mouth feel dry? Was I thinking of myself as physically unattractive as I performed? Was I afraid my audience thought I sounded stupid or incompetent? Answers to questions like this in written form provide the facts with which to make accurate judgments of how you are doing in overcoming your fears. Tracking your progress in writing will help you decide when you can proceed to more difficult exercises.

Everyone will have their own way of setting up such a record, but here's a sample first page to show how it might be done by someone working on public speaking:

EXERCISE 1: IMAGINING THE WORST
Leaping into real-life exercises may not be the best approach for many people, so I urge them first to try to imagine themselves, as

Date	Exercise	Symptoms	Anxiety Score	Notes
8/3/05	Spoke presentation alone	Racing heartbeat, some flushing	7	First time I've tried it. Not easy. Watched myself in mirror.
8/5/05	Spoke in front of a mirror again	Same symptoms	6	Seems a little easier, but every time I picture an audience, I start to get nervous.
8/6/05	Tried presentation in front of Jean	Slight heartbeat increase	4	Situation seemed a little artificial. Felt silly more than anxious.
8/8/05	Did presentation alone again	Terrible dry mouth	7	Decided to go back to presenting alone again. Tried hard to picture an audience. Did OK, but not great.
8/10/05	Got Jean to sit still for a repeat of the presentation	Almost none, but my mouth started to get dry toward the end	4	Felt more natural this time. Tried to pretend Jean was a stranger. Not sure if it worked.
8/11/05	Presentation in front of Jean and Kevin	Heart beating fast; fumbled with my words	7	Jean's suggestion to get Kevin involved. I started misreading and stuttering halfway through. Anxiety increased as I went along.

vividly as possible, in the anxiety-provoking situation that troubles them the most. Doing this can provoke the same physical and psychological symptoms as the real-life experience does, and practicing these mental exercises, unlikely as it may seem, can be the first step in getting the anxiety under control. The more you do these mental exercises, the less anxiety they will provoke. But you have to do them conscientiously, and since there's nothing especially pleasant about doing them, that won't be easy. I try to convince my patients that the exercises are important, and while my words may help, in the end you have to convince yourself they are worth the effort.

Suppose you dread returning something to a store. Try this:

1. Start by imagining your dissatisfaction with the purchase.
2. Then imagine walking back into the store with it.
3. Imagine speaking to a salesman to ask where the returns desk is.
4. Imagine approaching the returns desk and seeing the attendant waiting there.
5. Then invent an opening for your conversation with the woman at the desk.
6. Finally, imagine yourself putting the item on the counter and waiting for her to process your refund.

If you imagine these things vividly enough, you'll soon start to feel the physical symptoms you dread. But repeatedly imagining such a situation will dull the feelings—you'll get used to it. Getting used to thinking about it can be the first step in getting used to doing it.

EXERCISE 2: UNREALISTIC FEARS AND MALADAPTIVE BELIEFS

The rational part of your mind knows that there is nothing to fear in giving a well-prepared speech to a group, even a large group, of colleagues. But you fear the act anyway. Sometimes identifying and writing down such thoughts can expose them for what they are—improbable and irrational. Cognitive behavioral therapy aims at, among other things, eliminating exactly these kinds of irrational and self-destructive thoughts. You can do a little cognitive behavioral therapy on yourself with some simple exercises.

1. First imagine an anxiety-provoking thought and write it down: "If I stumble over a word in this speech, everyone will conclude that I'm an idiot."
2. Then ask yourself: "Is this a realistic idea? Is anyone who stumbles on a word in a speech necessarily an idiot?"
3. Finally, devise a way to expose the irrational thought for what it is: "I've heard lots of people, even the best public speakers, stumble over words. No one concludes that they're idiots. So if I stumble on a word, why would anyone conclude that I'm one?"

Here's another example:

1. "When I walk into a room full of people, everyone is looking at me."
2. "Is this really possible? Does everyone stop what they're doing to look up and stare whenever a person enters a room?"
3. "I noticed that John walked in a few minutes late to a large meeting, and no one even glanced at him. Is there really something especially noticeable about me that doesn't pertain to him? Obviously, no. So why would they stare at me if I did the same thing? The fact is, they wouldn't!"

Or again:

1. "Everyone in the restaurant notices that I'm a slob."
2. "Really? Is every single person in this restaurant concentrating on me rather than on what they're eating or their conversations with their dinner companions?"
3. "I know how to use a fork, and I chew with my mouth closed. I'm not interested in watching anyone else's manners, and they're not interested in watching mine. Anyway, I'm no neater or sloppier than anyone else. Thinking I am is completely irrational."

Whatever your specific fears are, you can create similar triptychs for your own use. Writing these thoughts down, along with the responses, can also be useful in checking your progress by reminding yourself of irrational or unrealistic beliefs.

EXERCISE 3: *IN VIVO* EXPERIENCE

In vivo (Latin for "in life") experience is the next step. This means facing your fears in real-life situations in a process called exposure therapy. This is a gradual process—no one is asking you to jump unprepared into the social situation you fear most. For example, perhaps you fear meeting and talking to new people at social gatherings— the very idea of going to a party where you won't know everyone makes your heart beat and your face flush.

First, set some modest goals, starting with actions that provoke the least anxiety and moving toward more difficult chores:

1. Go to a social gathering, stay for a short time. I don't have to directly talk to anyone. But I'll stay at least until my anxiety starts to decrease.

2. Go to a party and introduce myself to one person before leaving.
3. Stay at a social gathering for an hour, speaking to at least three people during that time.

You're going to feel anxious in approaching each of these exercises—no doubt about it. But you'll also begin to see that you can handle the anxiety, that it isn't going to hurt as much as you thought it would, and it certainly isn't fatal.

Be sure to write down your reactions and level of anxiety each time you try to achieve a goal. You don't have to succeed the first time—repeating an exercise is not a defeat. And even if you succeed once, you may fail the next time you try the same exercise. This is not unlike practice at a physical skill: you didn't succeed in riding a bicycle the first time you tried, either, and there was probably some fear and frustration before you did. But with practice, you learned to ride a bicycle. This kind of direct exposure to the situations the socially anxious person fears most, if done gradually and persistently, can eventually greatly reduce or eliminate the anxiety.

Succeeding once at any of the tasks you set for yourself is usually not enough. You have to be able to repeat the exercise successfully, and you have to be able to do it with a reduced level of anxiety. This means repeatedly putting yourself in the anxiety-provoking situation, rating your reactions, identifying weaknesses, and doing the exercise again. I told you it wasn't going to be easy.

❖ SMALL STEPS TOWARD
A BREAKTHROUGH

One of my own patients provides a good example of how exposure therapy works. Jason, fifteen years old at the time Ifirst saw him, had dropped out of high school—"I just couldn't take it anymore" was, at least at first, as much of an explanation I could elicit from him. Jason was a good student—that wasn't his problem. His parents, themselves well educated and conscientious about their son's intellectual development, were home-schooling him, and he was on a fairly aggressive medication program. The goal Jason and I agreed upon seemed simple enough: get back into the classroom and stay there.

I started out by asking him to go to one class—just sit in the back without saying anything. He could always, I promised, leave if the anxiety was too much for him. After a few false starts, he was able to sit through an entire class. Then, after a few weeks, he was able to go to a couple of classes in the same way. Math class was easier for him—the teacher didn't call on kids much, and he could avoid speaking in class. English was another matter: the first time the teacher started calling on people—not him, just people sitting near him—he became so frightened he wasn't able to go back to the class for several weeks. He could be redirected to other classes, but it took several more weeks to get him back to that English class. In any case, he was eventually able to graduate, although his inability to interact with other kids was always on his mind. He enrolled in a community college, living at home for the first year, and was able to perform adequately—that is, he could stay in class, felt no need to flee, and kept up with his work. He still had no friends, though. I asked him whether he could face going to the student center, just to be around other people, not necessarily to talk with them. He didn't even know where the student center was, but agreed to go online, find out its location, and then go over there for a visit. At first it was all he could do to walk through the place quickly. Then we agreed that he would try to stay there for a half hour or so, just to see what kinds of facilities they had. He found pool tables: perfect. We agreed he'd go over there, shoot some pool by himself, alone, without talking with anyone. The situation—playing pool alone in a crowded student center—was perfect to encourage social interaction. At first, he was only willing to go early in the day when there weren't many people around. Eventually, he was able to go at more crowded times, and finally succeeded in having a game with someone, the first social contact with another kid he'd ever had at school outside of a classroom. I kept telling him that he didn't have to be successful at these efforts—you can always decide to back out. But he was determined.

At this point, Jason was able to make a conscious choice to do something about his social isolation: he decided to move out of his parents' home, and, most important, find a roommate. I didn't suggest this—he did. This was one of those satisfying times in treatment where a patient makes a big leap after some small successes. Jason moved into a dorm with a roommate, a social situation he began to find natural and unforced. Jason is never going to be a social butterfly, but he's on his way to a normal and satisfying social life.

You've probably noticed the common theme in these exercises, whether the exercise is imaginary or real-life: each involves facing and experiencing your fears, even though at first it really hurts. It's common knowledge that when you fall off a horse, the best thing to do is to get right back on. Delaying only reinforces the fear. This is true of social situations as well. You probably have techniques for avoiding the situations that trouble you—you make excuses to avoid parties, never make a spontaneous remark in class, avoid public bathrooms, stay put in the same old job because you can't face a job interview, ensure that you'll never have to return anything to a store. And at the same time you know that in the end these tricks don't really serve your purposes but only make the fears harder to overcome, preventing you from leading the life you want to lead. But doing these exercises conscientiously, if necessary with the help of a trusted and understanding therapist, and abandoning your avoidance techniques can in the end provide heavenly relief from real pain.

Finding the Best Treatment

Compared with those who suffer from mental disorders of comparable severity, people with social anxiety disorder don't get much treatment. On average, a person suffers with social anxiety for fifteen years before seeking any professional intervention, and even then most people go to the doctor not because of their social anxiety, but because they are suffering from comorbid disorders like depression or panic disorder (see chapter 4). There are two explanations for this, one obvious and one not so. Obviously, people who suffer from social anxiety are more embarrassed about seeking professional help than others. Going to the doctor, dealing with the receptionist, sitting with other people in a waiting room, talking to people in authority—all these things are ordeals for the socially anxious, best delayed or avoided completely. But perhaps more fundamentally, people don't consider excessive shyness, even the crippling shyness of social anxiety, a mental disorder at all worthy of treatment.

Only about 5 percent of people with SAD seek help from a mental health professional. Even the expense of psychiatric treatment and its poor coverage in most insurance plans does not explain this. In Germany, for example, where all health care is free, a similarly low percentage of people suffering from SAD seek treatment. If there is another disorder involved, the percentage goes up to about 35 percent. But that's not the end of the problem. If you go to a general practitioner for help with SAD, 50 percent of the time he or she won't offer any effective treatment, won't send you to a specialist for another opinion, and in fact won't even recognize that you've got an illness.

Fortunately, this is changing. There are numerous organizations for people who suffer from anxiety disorders, and they have carried on significant publicity campaigns to help people understand the problem of social anxiety disorder. They emphasize first that it is a real disease, not just ordinary shyness, and second that there are effective treatments for it. These campaigns have had some success, and more people with SAD now seek treatment, but it is still true that most of these people have some other psychiatric problem that sends them to the doctor. I usually get my referrals from other doctors, but every once in a while someone comes in to see me after reading something published in print or on the Internet by one of these groups.

Mental Health Professionals: Navigating the Maze

It may be that people go to general practitioners for help with social anxiety at least partly because specialties in the mental health field are so confusing. Psychiatrists and other medical doctors, nurses, psychologists, social workers, mental health counselors, and therapists of many different kinds (sometimes depending on varying state licensing laws) all treat SAD as well as other mental illnesses. This proliferation of people providing mental health services leaves many patients confused about whom they should be consulting.

One of the most problematic aspects of this is that in most states almost anyone can hang out a shingle and call himself a "psychotherapist." Some states (New York, for example) are developing plans to license psychotherapists, but at present, psychotherapy is in most places pretty much a free-for-all. It is fairly easy and perfectly legal for an untrained or inexperienced person to provide psychotherapy. Since practicing *effective* psychotherapy requires both training and experience, this is not a good picture for consumers of mental health care. An unqualified psychotherapist, like an unqualified person in any health care field, can do considerably more harm than good.

In all states except New Mexico, only doctors who hold an M.D. degree and certain health professionals under their supervision may prescribe medicines for mental disorders. (In New Mexico, psychologists may also do so after undergoing a special training program.) A *psychiatrist* is a doctor with an M.D. degree who has undergone further training after medical school to specialize in psychiatry. This training usually consists of four years in a residency training program in a hospital, during which time the resident sees hundreds of patients under the supervision of senior staff members. To be board-certified, the doctor must then pass an examination administered by the American Board of Psychiatry and Neurology, which includes both a written portion and the clinical examination of one or more patients.

A *psychologist* usually has either an M.A. (master's degree) or a Ph.D. (doctoral degree) in psychology. Requirements for these degrees vary widely from one university to another, and even within the same university depending on what kind of psychology the recipient of the degree intends to practice. Usually a degree in clinical psychology indicates that the person has been trained in psychotherapy. Except in New Mexico, psychologists are not licensed to prescribe medicine, but they can and do perform effective psychotherapy while a medical doctor prescribes the medicine.

Social workers often practice psychotherapy and can be well qualified and highly expert. It is not an insignificant fact that their fees tend to be lower than those of psychiatrists. They don't prescribe medicine, but they often work with psychiatrists who do. Social workers, often called *psychiatric social workers,* provide more mental health treatment than any other specialty. These people generally have an advanced degree in social work—this can be an M.S. (master of science), an M.S.W. (master of social work), or a D.S.W. (doctor of social work). The National Association of Social Work tests and accredits social workers, and those who have undergone this accreditation process often write "A.C.S.W.," for Association of Certified Social Workers, after their names.

Nurses also practice psychotherapy. The title *psychiatric nurse* can be used to describe a nurse who works with psychiatric patients, but there are also *psychiatric nurse practitioners,* registered nurses who have additional specialty training in psychiatry. These practitioners, in many states, are licensed to prescribe medicine as well, and while many work in hospitals or clinics, others work independently in private practice.

Psychopharmacology, the science and practice of prescribing psychotropic medicines, is a complex and rapidly changing area of medicine, and not all medical doctors—not even all psychiatrists—are qualified to give the best care in this area. Ideally, medication for social anxiety, as for any other mental illness, should be prescribed and supervised by a *psychiatrist expert in psychopharmacology.* Outside of large cities, such specialists may be difficult to find, so in practice, much of the prescribing of these drugs is done by *general practitioners,* medical doctors who provide general family medical care. Although this may not be the best approach, it may be the only option for some people. If there are no specialists near you, it may be worth the time and expense to seek a consultation at an urban medical center with a psychiatrist who specializes in psychopharmacology. Most such centers have a referral service to help you find the right person. After a successful medication regimen is established, a local physician can continue to prescribe and monitor it.

Evaluating Social Anxiety Institutes and Programs

A number of groups give advice on or treat social anxiety disorder. Some are nonprofit organizations regulated or licensed by state health or education departments; others are privately owned profit-making companies. Many have fancy websites, which, as we know, does not guarantee good medical treatment. No judgment can be made about an organization simply on the basis of whether they are private or not; the only way to reach a conclusion about efficacy or expertise is by researching the particular program you're interested in. How to go about this research? Begin by asking, and getting satisfactory answers, to questions like these about the people providing treatment:

- Do the staff members have degrees from recognized institutions of higher learning?
- Are they nurses, social workers, psychologists, psychiatrists, or another recognized mental health professional?
- Are the physicians board-certified in psychiatry and neurology, or are they general practitioners with no specialist training in the area?
- If they are not psychiatrists, what special knowledge or experience do they have of psychiatric illness?
- What kinds of therapy do they use?
- How long have they been in practice?

Although many kinds of "talk therapy" can be used to treat social anxiety disorder, cognitive behavioral therapy (CBT) is a widely accepted and highly effective technique that can be practiced by any number of people with various degrees, or even no degree at all, and with many different levels of training. The only real qualification is expertise in the methods of CBT. Gaining this expertise, however, is not necessarily a simple matter, and the more experienced the therapist the better the treatment is likely to be. How can you tell who has experience and how well they have been trained in CBT?

One place to start would be the National Association of Cognitive Behavioral Therapists. This is an organization with missions in three areas: advocacy, teaching, and credentialing. It was formed in 1995 in response to the growing number of people who called themselves cognitive behavioral therapists but had no real training in its theory or practice. The NACBT sets standards for cognitive therapy and provides credentialing and certification based on those standards. Their board of advisors includes a number of widely published experts in the field, and their website offers referrals to therapists in your geographical area. Of course, not all good cognitive behavioral therapists are members of this organization, and many other kinds of therapy besides CBT are used for social anxiety.

Social Anxiety and the Family

When kids face difficult social situations, simply talking it over with their parents doesn't help. In fact, at least one study has found that discussing avoidant situations with their parents actually makes children's anxiety increase. But this doesn't mean that parents should be banned when their child has social anxiety. On the contrary, involving parents in treating children—in the right way—is essential. Parents can help in at least three ways: by rewarding and praising courageous behavior, learning to cope with their own anxiety, and helping with problem-solving skills. Parents often have exactly the same anxieties about social situations as their children do, and to the extent that they help their kids avoid social situations, they aren't helping solve the problem. I often have to ask parents to stand back, to let their children face situations on their own. In doing this, I'm not encouraging passive nonparticipation but making an active effort to help their kids face and solve their problems.

Although parents don't always have to have their therapeutic role formalized, there is at least one form of therapy specifically designed to teach parents how to play an important role in treatment. This is called family anxiety management, or FAM, and involves sessions with the kids and parents together, showing them strategies for reinforcement of good social behavior and for ignoring anxious behavior or complaints. Preliminary evidence shows that this approach is helpful in reducing anxiety and preventing relapse, and many parents will find a structured program like this useful.

These efforts by parents are important no matter what kind of therapy is being used to treat their children—the best therapy for a child is even more effective when the parents are wisely involved.

Ask a Professional

Often the best way to find the right therapist is to ask a trusted health care professional a simple question, for which the answer can almost always be helpful if you ask the right person: "Who would you go to if you had a problem like mine?" Even then, you may not find the best person the first time you try—a well-qualified psychotherapist might not be the right therapist for you. There are objective ways to determine qualifications, as we've described above, but deciding if you are comfortable with a given therapist is a decision you'll arrive at only by yourself.

Psychological Treatments for Social Anxiety

Although it is certainly not the only psychological treatment available, the usual first-line psychological treatment for social anxiety is cognitive behavioral therapy, sometimes called CBT, and many different kinds of mental health professionals use this method successfully. Psychologists, social workers, mental health counselors, and others—provided they are trained and experienced in its techniques—can all carry on effective cognitive therapy with patients who suffer from social anxiety. Of course, any therapist must first rule out physical illness as the cause of the anxious feelings. Any of a number of diseases can cause symptoms similar to anxiety attacks—thyroid illness, cardiac arrhythmias, mitral valve prolapse, adrenal tumor, among others—and treating a patient for social anxiety who is in fact suffering from, say, a heart condition, could be disastrous. A physical exam and laboratory tests to rule out such causes are a necessary prelude to any psychotherapy. Ruling out other psychiatric illnesses is just as important—so important, in fact, that I've devoted most of chapter 5 to that problem.

CBT: Correcting Errors in Thinking

Cognitive behavioral therapy is used to treat many different kinds of psychiatric problems. In treating social anxiety, the idea is that the irrational feelings of people who suffer from the disorder are victims of erroneous thinking, and that if they can understand that their feelings are based on false assumptions and irrational thoughts, they can reject those thoughts and rid themselves of the anxiety that follows. Once a patient understands that he is misconstruing his public experiences, he is on his way to conquering his fear.

For example, in trying to help the patient clarify his thinking, I might explain the physiological reactions to anxiety as what they are: normal bodily responses to fear, a biological reaction of the sympathetic nervous system. This reaction is controlled by the amygdala, a part of the brain that is the center of primitive flight or fight emotions that alert the body to threat before a full rational evaluation of that threat can be made. One idea in psychotherapy is to get the patient to use the prefrontal lobes, the part of the brain that controls rational thinking, to evaluate a threat before reacting to it. I might explain that the patient's fear has an evolutionary reason for existing— there was a time when such fears were essential to survival, though their appearance in, say, anticipating a public speaking engagement has clearly outlived its usefulness. This kind of explanation helps the patient realize that there is nothing "abnormal" about his fears, and that they can be consciously understood and consciously controlled. I can point out that what he is really feeling is the fear of a certain unpleasant sensation, not the fear of the public situation he is about to face. The distinction is both subtle and important. Nothing in the public speaking situation itself is innately dangerous or likely to harm him—giving a speech, he knows in the rational part of his mind, is not the same as walking a tightrope over Niagara Falls. Almost all socially anxious patients can acknowledge the irrationality of the fear itself. But at the same time, they are acutely aware of the emotional and physical pain they are going to experience when facing the necessity to give a speech. It is the anticipation of this pain—not the speech itself—that terrifies them. Being aware of the distinction is essential.

KEEPING IT SIMPLE

In CBT, the treatment is deliberately simple. I don't engage patients in long discussions about their backgrounds, their parents, their friendships, or their romantic relationships. Instead, we try to keep things specific and concrete. This means that I encourage the patient to discuss his fears in the most specific ways possible, something that is not easy for people with social anxiety. Here, the relationship between the patient and the therapist is critical. Unless there is a warm, trusting, and understanding relationship between therapist and patient, the patient will not be able to face and solve his problems. Many people see the doctor as an authority figure, someone ready to judge or evaluate them. A doctor working with a person with social anxiety cannot behave in this way. Instead, I model my interaction on that of a coach—the helpful coach version, not the shouting sadistic one. For an athlete to do his best, a coach needs to instruct him and encourage him to use the best techniques. The coach forms an alliance with the athlete, and together they pursue a common goal. A similar alliance between the therapist and the patient is essential, because the therapist has to get the patient to do the hard work of facing fear and tolerating anxiety. The patient has to know that he will feel worse before he feels better, and he has to trust the therapist to lead him through the process. Praise, even for small steps, is important.

I am not trying to change or improve my patient's personality with CBT—I couldn't do that even if I wanted to, which I don't.

What I want to do is make it easier for him to solve very specific problems and develop very specific social skills. The patient knows much more about himself than I do, and always will. I'm trying to understand things from his point of view. If I make a mistake—and believe me, I sometimes do—I admit it, correct it, and get on with the work we are trying to do together. This therapy is very much a collaboration.

What Happens in My Office

CBT involves teaching the patient to be aware of his thoughts, to see how they are distorted, and to use more rational ways of thinking. Sometimes the questions I ask are pretty simple: What do you gain by imagining that it's impossible for you to go to this party? What is the worst thing that can happen if you give this speech and make a mistake? What do you have to gain by overcoming your fear of talking on the telephone to a new business associate? I encourage the patient to ask himself these kinds of questions when facing an anxiety-provoking situation. I try to figure out what an individual's motivation for change is. It is essential for me to know what it is he wants to accomplish. What does he want to do that he finds himself unable to do now, and how can I help him do it?

I try to find out what is bothering the patient, clarify it so that we both understand the specifics, and then set out to find a solution. This means I don't want to cover a lot of issues in one session—two or three specific problems will be plenty. But I try to make sure these are major issues that are seriously impeding the patient in accomplishing his goals. Whether the goal is asking a woman out on a date, going to a party, getting married, having children, or anything else, present problems are the most important. I want to know what is bothering the patient right now and how we can find a solution immediately. There is, I always emphasize, no time like the present.

In CBT, I'm not interested in unconscious motivation. That's a different (though, as we will discuss, valuable) approach. In cognitive behavioral therapy, the therapist is more of a teacher, showing the patient methods of approaching situations he finds difficult to handle. As in any teaching situation, homework is important. Assigning specific tasks—making a phone call to someone you don't know well, facing the panic of entering the room when others are seated by doing just that—is essential. I urge my patients to try to surprise themselves with their ability to overcome fear.

❖ "HE TALKS, I WORK"

I once treated an electrician's assistant who was overwhelmed by performance-related issues, stymied by his inability to perform in even the most modest ways in public. Norm had held a job with the same company—working with the same boss—for more than twelve years. In his job, interacting with anyone except his boss was unnecessary, and this was in a way a good thing, since he was incapable of holding a job that involved social discourse. "The boss does the talking," he told me. "I do the wiring." This was a satisfactory arrangement for work, but in the rest of life you have to do the talking yourself. This he found almost impossible. He was unmarried, virtually friendless, and spent inordinate amounts of time at home alone or in solitary activities like going to the movies, even though he didn't seem particularly enthusiastic about movies. In fact, for a person who went to as many movies as he did, he seemed pretty down on the art form in general. Almost every time I ever asked him whether a particular film was worth seeing, his response was "Save your money." He had all the worst symptoms of social anxiety disorder, and they were destroying his life. As a homework assignment in therapy, I encouraged him to take an adult education class (it happened to have been a nonfiction writing class, but it could have been anything), and gave him the task of raising his hand in class to ask a question. Gradually, he became able to do this. He was older than most of the students in the class and began to discover that his knowledge and experience was helpful to younger students. Although he was terrified of taking a test, he found that helping younger students actually made him less anxious about his own exams. He discovered that he enjoyed being able to teach or tutor his classmates. His CBT homework assignments—taking an adult education class and speaking out in class—actually led to a profound change in his life: he is now studying for a degree in education and planning a career as a high school teacher.

MISTAKEN IDEAS

One aspect of social anxiety makes it starkly different from other phobias. A person who fears, for example, that a bridge he is driving on will fall down is unlikely to have his fear realized. Bridges don't collapse because a person fears they will. But for someone with social anxiety, the fear that he will be tongue-tied on a blind date is a realistic, and often realized, possibility. In fact, the fear of it helps realize the event. The probability of an airplane crashing is not increased by the fear that it will happen, but the probability of your mind going blank at a job interview is actually increased if you fear it, and this is especially true of those suffering from social anxiety. This is why changing the way a socially anxious person thinks can have a profound effect on what actually happens to her in daily life.

A number of studies show that people with social anxiety focus their attention on themselves in social situations to an extraordinary extent, and that this considerably impairs their ability to interact successfully. They can't even see in any realistic way how their audience is reacting—they're too busy focusing (usually negative) thoughts on themselves.

Another way in which the socially anxious person's thinking goes wrong is in believing that a poor performance at a public speech, for example, will have overwhelmingly negative and permanent effects on her life. In other words, she exaggerates the consequences of her fear to a point of irrationality. I sometimes mirror this process in therapy, inflating the disaster so greatly that it becomes ridiculous enough for even my patient to recognize its absurdity. For example, I had a middle-aged woman patient, a women's magazine editor, who thought everybody in any room she entered was judging her and coming to negative conclusions. Ironically, she was quite pretty, and there was nothing odd about the way she walked or presented herself; she was not, objectively, someone who would attract negative attention. Yet she was convinced that not only did she look stupid and awkward, but that her gauche presentation was so obvious that everyone in the room was staring at her. "Well," I said, "sure they are, every one of them. It's not only everybody in the room, but in the next room, too. And in the rest of the building. Even outside in the street," I said, pointing to the window, "everyone out there is thinking about nothing but you, and they're arriving at conclusions, too. It's not looking good for you. In fact," I added, now starting to smile with her, "the entire universe is concentrating on whether you are going to fall on your face as you walk into the room, and too bad for you when their decision comes down."

"Well," she said, now laughing, "maybe not quite everyone."

It is well-known that socially anxious people overestimate how evident their anxiety is to other people and overestimate how negatively their performance is viewed by others. Interestingly, this characteristic is not shared by people with other forms of anxiety or other psychiatric illnesses. It may be that the socially anxious person considers his internal state, his feelings, and the physiological reactions those feelings produce to be as obvious to others as they are to himself. The thumping heart, the feelings of blushing and heat, the sweating—he believes all these things are much more evident to other people than they in fact are. He assumes further that others are determined to evaluate him negatively, and he views the opinions of others—whatever their objective accuracy or value—as extremely important to his own well-being. A frown from an interlocutor, a sigh of boredom, a look of indifference however slight and however open to ambiguous interpretation, is construed as severe criticism. Any audience, whatever its size and however apparently benign, is a threat. Just walking down the street—where he suspects others may be watching him—is a reason for panic. Studies even show that people with social anxiety consider themselves less physically attractive than do people who are not so shy. This kind of thinking, moreover, dominates the mind of a person with social anxiety, distracting his attention from other tasks that might make his public performance easier or more effective. CBT aims to eliminate this kind of irrational thinking and substitute more rational and logical thoughts.

Going to School in CBT

CBT always involves a formal educational component. Patients learn about the nature of anxiety, its course, its causes, its physiological effects. They are also informed about the nature of cognitive behavioral therapy itself, that it is an active treatment and requires cooperation in the form of specific homework assignments.

CBT can be conducted in groups, which have certain advantages over individual therapy. First, most socially anxious people are relieved to learn that there are other people like them—otherwise perfectly normal people who suffer from this specific disorder. Sometimes patients feel liberated learning that there is actually a name and a treatment for their problem. In addition, the kinds of practice and reinforcement that go on in a group are extremely helpful. But for obvious reasons, many socially anxious people are not eager to participate in groups—after all, it is precisely public situations like these that provoke the anxiety that hobbles them.

Although there are many variations, CBT groups are usually about six or eight people with two therapists, one male and one female. Sessions last about two and a half hours. Usually, there is one session per week. The emphasis is on teaching people to recognize logical fallacies, mistaken ideas, automatic thoughts, and misinterpretations, and then to expose their irrationality. They hear about what works for other people—techniques that they can use to apply to their own fears. They get more realistic feedback about how irrational their thoughts are and get a more accurate picture of how much they are actually being scrutinized by others. They get support from the group as a whole and praise even for small successes, which are also opportunities for practicing social skills in a comfortable environment. Videotapes of real-life performances have also proven extremely useful, and people with social anxiety viewing tapes of themselves in public interactions often concede that their initial negative evaluation of their performance was inaccurate. This in itself helps to reduce anxiety.

CBT in Action

I have my patients rank the social situations that frighten them in order of most severe to least severe. Then I discuss the problems of irrational thoughts, whether people are really scrutinizing you or whether perhaps you exaggerate their interest in you. In this early period, I am developing an alliance with the patient, developing the trust that allows us to do successful work together.

Each person's motivation for change is different. There are often things that a person really wants to do but can't because of SAD. A relationship, a career move, a desire to have their kids involved in activities that their own social anxiety is preventing their children from doing. What the patient wants out of this therapy is not to be taken for granted. Often a patient has been living with the problem for a long time, so I want to know why he's coming in for treatment now. What does he want that SAD is preventing him from having?

I start a systematic program of homework. I might begin within the setting of my office, have her imagine being in a social situation, describe her level of anxiety in these imaginary situations, determine whether or not it's disabling, whether she can deal with that level of anxiety. We might progress from one kind of imaginal exposure to the next, each time having her describe a situation, role-play the situation, describe the negative thoughts, quantify the level of anxiety, talk about what she perceives as some of the possible negative outcomes of a social situation.

❖ MAKING BEAUTIFUL MUSIC

I had one patient, a thirty-four-year-old singer and guitarist of some fame who is comfortable when recording music but had severe anxiety in live-performance situations. In the therapy sessions, we listed different kinds of performance situations: playing at a party, playing at a small club, playing at a large concert hall. We quantified his anxiety associated with each on a scale of 1 to 10. Playing at a party might be a 4, playing in a club an 8, a concert hall a 10. I had him bring in his guitar (he actually had three different guitars, one of them a 12-string, and would bring them in in turn) and perform in the therapy setting. At first he just performed for me, describing his level of anxiety as he played, the negative cognitions, whether he was being scrutinized, evaluated, judged, and what he thought the consequences of such an evaluation might be. We worked our way through four different settings—therapy, party, club, concert hall. First he imagined these different situations rating each one. Then we did some role-playing, where he would do the performance but we would set up situations that would remind him of the actual locale. Then I sent him out to perform for a few friends in a protected club environment; then he went to a club where he didn't know people; each time, he gained a sense of mastery and habituated to the level of anxiety. He needed lots of support and encouragement about his progress, and I gave it to him. Gradually, this changed the way he thought about his performances and altered his level of focus so that he no longer focused on groups of people but concentrated on one individual he was playing to. With each successive level, he could imagine himself performing only to one person, reducing the amount of anxiety. While all this practice was going on, I prescribed a beta-blocker that eliminated many of the physical symptoms of anxiety. Once he got some success and a greater level of comfort, he was able to play in public without the use of the medicine.

Then I like to have the patient face the actual situation, starting with the easiest. What level is the easiest? That's up to the patient. This is practice—it's not important where you start. I urge patients to explain exactly what it is that frightens them: "Everybody thinks I'm stupid." "I'm going to humiliate myself." "Everyone will see that I'm incompetent." By this I'm trying to get the patient to look at the situation more realistically.

Facing the situation involves lots of support and reinforcement, and having them stay in the situation until the anxiety starts to dissipate. I try to explain that anxiety isn't gong to overwhelm you: you can get used to it, you can stay with the situation. With each practice situation, the patient gains confidence.

Exposure Treatment

Exposure treatment is often a part of CBT. The theory behind this technique is that exposure to the feared situation actually decreases anxiety by habituation—just like getting used to cold water when you go swimming. But we don't simply thrust people into a social situation and let them sink or swim. Instead, we create controlled situations in which the anxiety can be experienced without fear of negative consequences. One way is simply to imagine the feared social situation as vividly as possible and in great detail. Another is for the therapist and patient to act out a social situation, each playing a role. The third way is actual exposure in a real-life social encounter. By working through these progressive steps, the patient can learn to handle the anxiety. This technique has long been recognized as effective, and it is often viewed as a necessary component of cognitive behavioral therapy.

Every patient is different, and an individual program has to be worked out with each. There are no one-size-fits-all solutions. The first step is to develop an "exposure hierarchy"—that is, a list of social interactions in order of how much anxiety they cause, a kind of top-ten list of feared situations (although no need to have exactly ten of them!). For example, a patient might list his fears in this order: public speaking, talking to people in authority, meeting strangers, taking a test, telephoning in public. I might start by proposing that the patient and I act out a situation in which he is making a telephone call while I am a bystander. The patient who trusts his therapist will recognize that this role-playing can have no negative consequences, yet at the same time it will provoke some of the same feelings of anxiety he would feel in a real-life situation. Overcoming those anxieties in this controlled atmosphere is practice for overcoming them in the real world. Once this role-play is mastered in the moderately feared situation of making the phone call, we can move on to other, more anxiety-provoking scenarios.

Here's how it works in practice. I had a patient who was a modestly successful actor, the kind you've seen several times in different movies or TV shows but you can't seem to remember his name. His growing performance anxiety was taking a toll on his career, seriously starting to hold him back. First I had him imagine himself doing a performance. He was easily able to provoke the same feelings and physiological reactions he experienced during an actual performance, but now was able to practice getting them under control. When he was able to do this, he enrolled in a dramatic theory class (his idea, not mine), where there are no actual performances, but where there would be contact with a group of other students of similar interests. After doing this successfully, he attended an acting class where performance is part of the course. In the controlled and largely supportive atmosphere of the classroom, he was gradually able to control the symptoms that had been paralyzing him. Finally, we were able to arrive at a point where he could go to an actual audition—the most stressful event he could conceive of—and successfully control his symptoms and perform at his best. This quick summary exaggerates the speed at which all this occurred—it is not a quick process by any means, and there were many fits and starts. In fact, during one four-month period, he cut about half his classes and refused to attend any auditions at all. But it was in the end successful.

Often people in the performing arts can be quite comfortable on stage—adopting a role—and yet suffer from SAD in private situations. It's not only performance artists who do this—doctors can, too. Doctors are not immune to anxiety, but in stressful situations we can adopt our roles as doctors, which gives us a sort of script to follow. When I meet a patient, I have an almost automatic procedure—not that I've written it down, I do it by habit. I become the doctor, a role I obviously don't take on in other interactions with people in my life. Since I have this role as a kind of armor, it smoothes out the social interaction for me. Often performers described as "aloof" may be suffering from a form of SAD—they seem aloof only because in a personal interaction they have no clear role to adopt. Suddenly, they are at a loss.

Social Effectiveness Therapy: Learning Social Skills

Social Effectiveness Therapy (SET), sometimes called social skills training, was developed about twenty-five years ago, and it came, as many new therapies do, with great promise as the quick and easy cure for all sorts of psychological problems. We now recognize that it is valuable in treating social anxiety and other disorders, but only in conjunction with other therapies, and only in the hands of a skilled therapist. It is a tool, not a panacea, and it isn't useful for all patients with social anxiety. But for some, it works quite well.

The key element in SET is social skills training. Social skills—the wide range of verbal and nonverbal behaviors involved in successful interactions with other people—seem to come naturally to most people, but often not to those with social anxiety. These skills, so ordinary to most people as to hardly merit the term "skill," include eye contact, posture, tone of voice, use of gestures, clarity of speech, and other behaviors, all monitored, adjusted, and readjusted during social interactions as the demands of the situation change. The apparently simple act of asking for directions from a stranger, for example, requires a subtle blending of all of these actions into the suitable performance that constitutes a successful social interaction. The inability to do this can paralyze a person with social anxiety. She can't perform the task because she doesn't have the skills. But these skills can be taught, and that is the point of social skills training.

If you analyze any ordinary social interaction carefully, you can see that it requires a quite complex combination of skills, and you can understand why not everyone is in firm possession of them. Take starting a conversation with someone you've never met, for example. Your eye contact has to be appropriate—you can't be glancing around the room or over the shoulder of the person you're addressing, but at the same time you don't want to stare at him as if you were trying to drill a hole in his head with your eyes. You need the right body posture—open, not defensive, a stance that lets your interlocutor know you want to hear what he has to say. You have to maintain a certain physical distance, neither too close nor too far away. Even the angle at which you hold your head can be significant to the person you're speaking with. Your voice has to be modulated and your words have to be chosen in exactly the right way depending on whom you are trying to address—you don't want to speak to a policeman in the same tone or with the same vocabulary that you would use with a four-year-old child. Your facial expression has to be appropriate, and if you are going to gesture, the gestures have to fit the situation. You have not only to listen when the other person talks, but convey to that other person that you have heard and understood, which requires not only vocalization but just the right subtle combination of body language, head movements, and postures. And while you're doing all this, you have to be monitoring yourself and the other person, constantly making adjustments as circumstances change. Imagine the varying subtle requirements of the numerous social situations we face all the time—a job interview, asking for a date, getting directions from a passerby, talking to a policeman when you're about to get a speeding ticket, negotiating a disagreement with a salesperson, comforting a child, starting a conversation with a stranger at a cocktail party, offering help to someone, greeting a coworker, and a thousand others—all requiring different vocabulary and tones of voice, different gestures, facial expressions, and postures. Plus, you need to blend all of these in carefully timed and varying ways. You can see how difficult such interactions can be and how much expertise they require.

Social Skills Training in Practice

How social skills training is carried out varies, but the variations share certain characteristics. We teach behavioral skills by instruction and example, often with role-playing as a means of practicing. The therapist might, for example, play the role of a college student, asking the patient to approach and begin a conversation with a fellow student who happens to be sitting next to him in his first class. As the patient begins the dialogue, the therapist helps him interpret social cues—hearing and interpreting a tone of voice, a posture, a facial expression—in other words, getting him to consciously notice and practice the things socially adept people do more or less instinctively. Then the therapist can watch as the patient monitors himself, helping him to react properly to the cues his role-playing interlocutor is offering. If the patient speaks too loudly, approaches too closely, or shies away inappropriately, the therapist can correct him, modeling how people communicate successfully both verbally and nonverbally and demonstrating how the patient can do the same. Gradually, the patient learns these indispensable social skills in the same way he learns other tasks and then works on deploying them properly in various situations. Social effectiveness therapy, like cognitive therapy, is typically about fifteen two-hour appointments, or even fewer and shorter sessions.

The teaching in social effectiveness training is carried on essentially in the same way you teach any skill—by modeling, practicing, correcting, reinforcing the right behavior, and discouraging the wrong. Practice, as in learning any skill, is essential, and the more you practice the better you get. Often the therapy is conducted in groups, where there is ample opportunity to practice skills with others. The group leader may, for example, say, "Let's imagine that this group is a cocktail party, and you have to start a conversation with the person standing next to you." An exercise like this, in which many people can participate simultaneously to create a realistic but controlled situation offers patients the opportunity to practice managing their anxiety while carrying out the required task. Feedback and reinforcement, common to the success of many learning tasks, are also essential in social effectiveness therapy. The therapist or the group provides both encouragement and correction.

Practicing Social Skills in Real Life

With both cognitive therapy and social effectiveness therapy it has been clearly shown that practice in the group or with an individual therapist is not enough to provide lasting effects, so practice as homework in the real world (*in vivo* exposure) is also essential. While both cognitive behavioral therapy and social effectiveness therapy use exposure, the goal is slightly different in each. In cognitive therapy, *in vivo* exposure is usually short and is designed to correct irrational thinking. In SET, on the other hand, the exposure is much longer and the goal is habituation, not the correction of erroneous thought patterns. The therapist may set a task: buy something in a store, and then, a day later, return it. The patient tries this interaction by himself in the real world, records his responses or self-evaluation after performing the task, and reports to the therapist or the group on the results of his efforts. Of course, it isn't always this easy to construct in real life the specific situation that causes anxiety in a given patient. It may be difficult or impossible for a man who is afraid of speaking up at a business meeting to create that situation often enough on command. In such cases, role-playing is the best substitute. This creates the same increase in anxiety, and even though it may not be of the same intensity, it can be enough to create a therapeutic effect with repeated exposure.

Some studies show that exposure homework alone is enough to effect considerable improvement in patients with social phobia. An Italian study treated a group of socially anxious patients with exposure therapy alone, without the therapy sessions and continuing guidance that formal CBT involves. Each patient simply developed with the therapist a list of graded exposures to anxiety-provoking situations which he or she then carried out, carefully recording responses. The treatment lasted eight sessions, and in several cases it was so successful that patients were able to reduce or discontinue their drug regimens. A one-year follow-up examination showed that the changes had persisted, and that most patients had undergone even further improvement. This was a small study—only ten patients were involved, so we have to be careful in drawing large conclusions from it—but the results were compelling. The authors of the study also point out that each program was worked out carefully with each individual patient; the procedure was not simply generic encouragement to face social situations or some sort of preprogrammed instruction sheet. A person may have a diagnosis of social anxiety, but that does not define his personality or illuminate his human qualities.

Cognitive behavioral therapy works for social anxiety, and studies have demonstrated its effectiveness. It has been shown to be more effective than placebo (sugar pill) and more effective than controls placed on waiting lists. And there is also evidence to support the long-term effectiveness of behavioral therapy, including at least one study that showed continued effectiveness as long as five years after the therapy had ended. But I hope I haven't made CBT sound like the be-all and end-all for social anxiety, because it isn't. It has plenty of limitations. First, not everyone wants to participate in this kind of therapy. It's easy to imagine a person who would find the required activities inconvenient, bothersome, or otherwise unappealing. And for a certain percentage of people the therapy simply doesn't work even if they do try it. Moreover, even when therapy—any therapy—does work, it isn't the end of the story. SAD is a disorder that starts in early adolescence, and if you've been restricted in your social interactions since that age, you need time to catch up with your social skills. Maybe you don't feel anxious anymore, but that doesn't mean that you can immediately go to a cocktail party and have smooth and interesting conversations with a half-dozen strangers. You don't suddenly gain the ability to breeze through complex social situations just because you no longer feel the anxiety that such situations used to provoke. You still need time to develop skills and techniques, and this takes longer than the few weeks of cognitive behavioral therapy that were so helpful in reducing your anxiety.

Other Psychological Therapies for Social Anxiety

Not all patients respond to the conventional kinds of behavioral therapy for social anxiety, so for these patients the search for relief continues. There are other therapies, some with long histories and well studied, others newer and less carefully examined, that have been effective in treating people with SAD. These range from one of the oldest forms of talk therapy, psychoanalysis, to some treatments that might be called alternative. The term "alternative" has a bad reputation in medicine because it is often used to refer to treatments that are unscientific, untested, unproven, or sometimes even dangerous. And it has a New Age ring to it that makes most doctors pretty uncomfortable. But let's use the term to describe some kinds of treatments, both professionally administered and self-guided that, although not necessarily strictly scientific or systematically studied, seem to work for some patients, and certainly don't appear to do any harm.

Psychoanalysis

Psychoanalysis based on Freudian theory is perhaps the oldest form of talk therapy, and it undoubtedly has some usefulness in treating social anxiety. Classical "drive theory" posits that social anxiety as well as other kinds of anxiety are caused by a conflict between the id and the superego. In social anxiety, the anxiety caused by an unacceptable sexual or aggressive wish is displaced onto an otherwise neutral object—in this case, public performance of some kind. The anxiety occurs because the public performance triggers repressed conflicts about sexuality or aggression. Later psychoanalytically based theories, such as object relations and interpersonal approaches, theorize that the anxiety springs from a broader range of emotional needs (for example, the need for acceptance or approval), which are manifested in the public performance situation. It is, in other words, not the public act itself but the lack of a sense of security about approval and acceptance that provokes the anxiety. In these theories, the source of the insecurity is often traced to an overprotective parent.

Social anxiety is by definition a social problem. But psychoanalysis, at least in its traditional form, concentrates on the individual, not his social interactions. Inborn drives and internal mechanisms of defense, not external interactions, are at work, and the individual is not consciously aware of these psychic activities. Other people are objects of the expression of these drives. This traditional theoretical structure has been modified in certain ways with later developments in psychoanalytic thinking, but in general psychoanalysis does not usually concern itself with social interaction as an independent phenomenon.

Yet the problem of SAD doesn't exist all by itself without reference to other psychological phenomena—it isn't a broken arm that, once treated and healed, no longer affects you. If you're reading this book, you probably have suffered for some time with SAD. You've acquired habits and attitudes that are an integral part of the way you live, and you started acquiring them very early on. Studies show that early environment plays a role in predisposing people to social anxiety, and examining your past relationships can be a powerful tool in understanding why you feel the way you do. So before we dismiss psychoanalysis as old-fashioned or unscientific, let's pause a moment.

The scientific evidence for its effectiveness is, admittedly, weak. But the scientific evidence for the effectiveness of other psychological therapies, including CBT, is also weak, so it's difficult to condemn psychoanalysis on that basis alone. At my hospital, our resident physicians—all of them trained in medical school in the techniques and practices of science, knowledgeable about scientific methods, many of them engaged in scientific research projects that have nothing to do with psychoanalysis—still find psychoanalytic theory one of the most interesting and useful parts of their training. Whatever weaknesses its theoretical underpinnings contain, and however seemingly impractical its demands in money and time, in practice psychoanalytic psychotherapy has been shown to be very helpful in treating patients with many different kinds of psychiatric disorders, including SAD. How can this be explained? A difficult question to answer, but here's my shot at it.

A person in cognitive behavioral therapy doesn't have much of a choice—there's a plan and a schedule, and whatever adjustments are made in the plan are usually minor changes to homework or exercises or timing. Details aside, the overall plan is pretty much the same for everyone. The therapist, or the program, shows the patient the way. In psychoanalysis, on the other hand, it's the patient who is in charge. If other therapies aren't much interested in what the patient has to say about the way he feels, psychoanalysis is. From the patient's point of view, the analyst isn't applying a "technique" at all—he's just listening to what the patient has to say. If I'm the patient in a psychoanalytically oriented therapy, I'm in charge of what's to be considered important and what we're going to talk about. While psychoanalytic theory helps the therapist listen, inquire, organize his thoughts, and guide the process of therapy, the theory doesn't matter to me if I'm the patient. The only valid conclusions about myself are the ones I reach myself. Psychoanalysis provides a way of thinking about my subjective experience that behavioral therapies do not. As subconscious feelings are examined, exposed, and interpreted, I can learn to deal with them in a more constructive manner than by allowing the anxiety they provoke to cripple me in public situations.

PSYCHOANALYTICALLY ORIENTED PSYCHOTHERAPIES

Other kinds of therapy, though not strictly psychoanalytic, nevertheless incorporate some parts of psychoanalytic theory. In supportive therapy, the therapist tries to communicate a feeling of warmth and security within the therapeutic relationship, with the therapist interacting much more with the patient than in traditional psychoanalysis. Client-centered therapy is another variation of this type of supportive treatment.

Interpersonal therapy (IPT) assumes that most problems stem from failures in interpersonal relations, and such a theory would seem custom-made for the treatment of a disorder like social anxiety, whose interpersonal aspects are its most obvious component. This type of therapy was originally developed to treat depression, but it has been modified to treat other types of psychiatric disorder as well. In IPT, there is no delving into the past for the roots of problems. Instead it focuses on the present situation and specific problems in an attempt to alleviate symptoms. In treating social anxiety disorder, conflicts in relationships with friends, coworkers, bosses, and significant others are the central issues. This is a brief therapy (usually a few months), and it is done individually.

UNCONVENTIONAL THERAPIES

With hypnosis and eye-movement desensitization (EMDR) treatments, we are perhaps coming to the outer edge of realistically effective approaches to social anxiety disorder. One anecdotal report (that is to say, not a scientific study) of using a combination of hypnotherapy and biofeedback to treat a difficult case of social anxiety might be of interest, and hypnosis has been used to treat social anxiety with some reported success, but there are no controlled studies demonstrating its effectiveness or long-term outcome and some have suggested that hypnotherapy may prove more a way of avoiding social situations than of successfully approaching them. EMDR, a controversial treatment that involves desensitization by imagining social interactions in as vivid a way as possible, is likewise poorly studied as a treatment for social anxiety, although it has had some apparent success in treating post-traumatic stress disorder. I don't use hypnosis or EMDR, and I know few doctors who do. They're not well tested scientifically; there is little evidence that they work in any consistent way. I don't condemn these approaches—they are unlikely to do any serious harm to anyone, and for some people they might actually work. But I don't entirely trust them, either. I mention these treatments here more to acknowledge their existence than to recommend them.

Self-Help for Social Anxiety

Self-help techniques for social anxiety vary from books (like this one), videotapes, and CDs to formally organized programs like Dale Carnegie courses or, one of the most famous, Toastmasters International.

Toastmasters International is a nonprofit corporation founded in 1924 as a self-help organization for people who want to perfect their ability to speak in public. Anxiety about public speaking is probably the most common complaint of anxious people (not all of whom are suffering from social anxiety disorder), so the program has proven useful to many. Reducing anxiety is a significant though not the only part of the program. Groups usually meet weekly to practice public speaking and get feedback from other members. With twenty to thirty people in a group, each meeting gives all attendees the opportunity to practice conducting meetings and giving short impromptu or prepared speeches. Each speaker is assigned an evaluator who points out strengths and weaknesses and makes suggestions for improvement. This is, in a way, similar to the exposure therapy described earlier, and therapists treating patients with social anxiety often recommend Toastmasters as a good controlled situation for homework in confronting the problem of public speaking. People with severe cases of social anxiety probably cannot tolerate going to such meetings, but as an adjunct to other kinds of therapy, the program can be quite useful. Becoming a member and attending meetings costs about $75 per year. There are about 190,000 members in 9,500 clubs in 78 countries. Although you might imagine that politicians serving in public office are among those least likely to need help with public speaking, there are Toastmasters clubs in the U.S. Senate and the House of Representatives.

≈

Workbooks are often recommended as supplementary material for people in treatment with behavioral therapists. A selection is listed in the Resources section. People who because of their illness avoid any other kind of treatment may find these materials educationally useful.

≈

Since we use personal computers for almost everything else in our lives, it was inevitable that CD-ROMs would be appropriated for use in self-help for social anxiety. Computers have also been used to create virtual reality programs that can cause the same kind of response as real-life anxiety-provoking situations, but this area is brand new, and it isn't clear how this kind of activity would be incorporated into more conventional treatments.

Virtual reality programs are now used in treating the fear of heights, public speaking, and other specific phobias, and although I know of none for social anxiety, it is easy to imagine that some could be developed. Virtually Better, a company in Decatur, Georgia, has a clinic in which virtual reality therapy is carried on. The patient wears goggles and watches a computer-generated interactive scene that realistically reproduces the feared situation. They have produced programs that re-create glass elevators and bridges to simulate the fear of height, computer-generated audiences to reproduce public speaking situations, and virtual reality airplane cabins to treat the irrational terror of flying. The company is experimenting with vibrating platforms to simulate movement and even with chemically created odors to make the scenes more lifelike. In addition to running their own clinic, staffed by technicians and psychologists, Virtually Better leases equipment to clinicians and researchers. The equipment and the fees charged patients to use it are in general considerably higher than for conventional kinds of therapy.

There isn't much in the way of scientific evidence that these programs are effective, but it's hard to see how it would harm anyone to try them, and there are certainly personal testimonies that they work. The same is true for such activities as Internet chat groups and e-mail—no one knows whether such activities, which might be more comfortable for people suffering from social anxiety, will actually translate into improved functioning in the real world.

The Next Step in Treatment

There are at least two practical problems with psychological treatments for social anxiety. First, the treatment is often expensive and almost always time-consuming. Even the briefest of treatments lasts several months, and costs begin to mount very quickly. Second, in many places outside of large cities, there aren't enough trained therapists to carry out the treatment. In addition, medicine sometimes works better than psychotherapy for certain people, and often the two together are the best treatment of all. Drug therapy for psychiatric diseases has developed rapidly over the past two decades, and medicine for social anxiety is our next topic.

Pharmacological Treatments for Social Anxiety

Not everyone likes the idea of taking medicine for psychiatric illnesses. Even people willing to concede that psychiatric illnesses exist and are treatable sometimes resist the idea of drug treatment. They think of medicine as a "crutch" that doesn't resolve the root causes of a disease. Taking a pill to overcome shyness, even the severe and debilitating shyness of social anxiety, makes some feel that they are taking medicine for something they should be able to resolve on their own through strength of character. The idea that the brain can have a psychiatric disease treatable with a pill strikes some as a denial of their individuality or an intolerable interference with their free will. But if you think about the brain as a biological organ, however complex and poorly understood, there is little reason to hold this position. After all, eyeglasses are a "crutch" too, but no one is asking you to correct your vision by an act of will. And discovering the "root cause" of a psychiatric illness, as interesting or productive as that may be, is surely not as important or as urgent as getting relief from serious symptoms that cause considerable distress and are interfering with having the life you want. Knowing the root causes of your problem doesn't always make things better.

I had a patient, a prosecuting attorney, who came to me complaining of his fear of speaking in court—an obviously crippling problem given his profession. He was fine in other social situations, even in some that required public speaking, but in court he would freeze up despite determined efforts to prepare himself for every possible interaction with the judge, the witnesses, and the other lawyers. I thought medication could help, but he didn't want any, so we started a program of psychotherapy. And talk therapy did help him considerably. His relationship with his wife improved, he was happier in his work, he even managed to improve his relationship with his two teenaged children, one of whom he had been having a tough time with for many reasons. Unfortunately, it didn't help him with his chief complaint: he was still terrified of saying the wrong thing in court. Finally, I convinced him to try 75 mg of Effexor once a day after breakfast, a fairly small dose. Within three weeks, his fear of appearing in court had disappeared. Okay, this isn't a typical case, and while this man certainly had a psychiatric illness, it probably was not social anxiety. But the case illustrates the ways in which talk therapy can be useful for many important things while medicine does something else entirely but equally helpful.

Another objection to the use of psychotropic drugs comes in the form of a political or economic belief that drug companies are "inventing" diseases, and then pushing pills for them not because they have any beneficial effect but because they make money by selling them. They "medicalize" shyness and, in league with doctors, give it a scientific-sounding name, social anxiety disorder, in order to increase profits.

Obviously, drug companies benefit when they can find a medicine that treats a disease, and the reputation of the pharmaceutical industry is such that it is understandable that people might suspect them of scheming to make more money. But the Food and Drug Administration (FDA) actually makes it very difficult for a drug company to get approval to sell a drug. The FDA requires that the drug company establish that the drug is safe and effective before they will give approval for its sale, and requirements for proving this scientifically are extremely strict. They require many studies and tests, both with animals and people, and extremely complex analyses of the data on both efficacy and safety before any approval is given. Even after the drug is approved and marketed, there is after-market testing to see how the drug works in practice, and many drugs having gone through the long process of getting approval have been withdrawn from sale because of problems discovered only after hundreds of thousands of people have used them. The entire process of obtaining approval to sell a drug almost always costs tens of millions of dollars and takes many years to complete. Then, if the company wants to get a drug like Zoloft, which was originally developed to treat depression, approved for a new use, such as treating social anxiety disorder, even more testing and studies are required.

Of course, doctors are still free to prescribe drugs for unapproved uses, and none of this means that drug companies don't like to make money, and the more the better. It is also safe to say that none of them is immune to venality or greed, which may lead some of them to falsify, or at least exaggerate, the beneficial effects of the products they're selling. But putting aside our suspicions about the motivations of drug companies and looking at the scientific evidence gives us another picture: psychotropic drugs work, and they have provided, and continue to provide, relief to people suffering from some of the most painful diseases known to medicine, substantially improving their level of performance and their satisfaction with their lives.

The drugs discussed below have all been studied and used in the treatment of social anxiety, even though the FDA has not approved most of them for this purpose. This "off label" use of drugs by a physician is both legal and ethical. In the last couple of years, the Food and Drug Administration has approved several new drugs for the treatment of social anxiety, removing them from the "off label" use category. The FDA approved them for the same reason they approve any new drug: because they have been proven safe and effective.

The complex, time-consuming, and very expensive process of gaining approval for a drug involves a series of studies culminating in placebo-controlled trials. In these trials, large numbers of people, matched for, among many other things, their age, general health, and the severity of the illness under study, are divided into two groups. One group takes the medicine, one group takes a placebo, or sugar pill. The pills look alike, the bottles they come in look the same, and neither the patients nor the people administering them know who is taking the medicine and who is taking the placebo. (This information is concealed in codes kept by people not involved with the administration of the pills.) Over a given period of time, the results are observed and recorded and then the code is broken. If the people taking the medicine on average get significantly better than those taking the sugar pill, then the medicine is considered effective. It sounds simple and straightforward enough when explained this way, but it is a process that involves a series of complex decisions and statistical calculations, and even then definitive conclusions are not always possible. In any case, much has been learned in recent years about the effectiveness of various psychiatric medicines in treating social anxiety.

Prescribing and using these drugs is not simple. You may respond quite differently from someone else to the same medicine in exactly the same dose. Some people need small doses, some larger. Some will suffer serious side effects, others a few minor ones or none at all. Little is known about how to predict these variations. Often the beneficial effects aren't felt until the patient has been using the drugs for several weeks, and sometimes the side effects are felt before the therapeutic effects, which discourages people from continuing with them. Patients will refuse to start the medicines, or stop taking them after they have started, for both good and bad reasons, and it is up to the prescribing physician to establish a collaborative relationship strong enough to work with a patient to provide the best possible treatment. A doctor can't just give these pills to people, tell them to "take them for a few weeks," and then hope for the best. If she does, the patient may forget or simply choose not to follow the doctor's instructions for taking them. Or the patient might just stop taking them entirely. In either case, the chances that the drugs won't work will be vastly increased.

Although general and family practitioners are the most frequent prescribers of psychotropic medication, the best person to prescribe these drugs is a psychiatrist, particularly one who has training and experience in psychopharmacology, a complex and rapidly changing area of medicine.

Selective Serotonin and Serotonin-Norepinephrine Reuptake Inhibitors

The selective serotonin reuptake inhibitors (SSRIs) and the closely related serotonin-norepinephrine reuptake inhibitor called Effexor (venlafaxine) were first developed to treat depression but have been found to be useful for various anxiety disorders, including social anxiety. Three of them—Paxil, Zoloft, and Effexor—have received FDA approval for the treatment of social anxiety disorder, and even those without specific FDA approval for this purpose are often prescribed by physicians to treat the disorder. They are now considered the first-line pharmacological treatment for social anxiety.

Why do they work? As with many other psychotropic medicines, establishing *why* they work is much harder than establishing *that* they work. The action of these drugs is not completely understood, but they function at nerve endings, where nerves connect to each other to pass signals within the brain. Signals between nerves are carried both by electrical impulses and by chemicals called neurotransmitters. Serotonin is one of these; norepinephrine is another. These chemicals are released at the nerve endings and then are dispersed in various ways. They can be taken up by the neighboring nerve cell, decomposed by enzymes, or taken up by the same nerve that released them. The SSRIs, it is believed, reduce the ability of the nerve to "reuptake" serotonin (or norepinephrine in the case of Effexor), allowing levels of these transmitters to build up at the nerve endings—thus the term "reuptake inhibitors." No one knows exactly how, but these neurotransmitters are involved in controlling moods (among other bodily functions such as temperature, sleep, and appetite) and inhibiting their reuptake relieves the symptoms of various depressive and anxiety disorders.

All of these drugs have side effects, which we discuss below, but they are generally minor, they don't occur in everyone, and when they do occur they often fade after a short period of time. If side effects persist, there's a sure way to avoid them: stop taking the drug. In other words, the drugs may not always provide complete relief, but they almost never make things worse. It is almost always worth sticking with a drug for several weeks before deciding it is not for you.

One important warning about SSRIs at the outset: these drugs should never be used in combination with MAO inhibitors (brand names Nardil, Parnate, Eldepryl, and Marplan), which are sometimes used to treat depression. If you are taking MAO inhibitors, you must be off them for at least two weeks before starting an SSRI. Although alcohol isn't necessarily dangerous if taken with SSRIs, it can be a problem in that it can add to the side effect of sleepiness. Some psychiatrists believe that SSRIs can actually enhance the effect of alcohol. So it's probably a good idea to stay away from alcohol while using these drugs, at least until you're absolutely sure that you remain completely alert when taking them.

Medications Specifically Indicated for SAD

PAXIL

Paxil, or paroxetine, was the first drug approved for the treatment of social anxiety disorder. A 12-week double-blind controlled study testing Paxil against a placebo showed clearly that moderate social anxiety responded well to Paxil and that severe social anxiety responded even better. The differences were clear within two weeks after the start of the tests, and increased over the course of the study: 69 percent of patients responded to Paxil, and 29 percent to the placebo.

People who had other diseases in addition to social anxiety were not included in the study, so the results say nothing about how comorbid problems might be affected by taking this medicine. But Paxil is also approved for treating depression, obsessive-compulsive disorder, and panic disorder. No one is claiming that Paxil is a cure-all, but it is certainly likely that people who have social anxiety along with any of these other psychiatric disorders could gain broad benefits from using it.

Several other placebo-controlled tests of Paxil have been undertaken, and all have shown about the same effectiveness in using the drug for social anxiety. The usual dose is 20 mg a day, although occasionally patients may receive higher doses of 40 mg and 60 mg. When researchers looked at the effect on subgroups selected by age, race, and gender, they found no differences in effectiveness.

Paxil has been used for years to treat social anxiety, even though it was only approved by the FDA for depression. So why did its manufacturer, GlaxoSmithKline, bother to get approval for this use from the FDA? In 1999, the company spent $31.5 million promoting it—but not for social anxiety, which would have been illegal. Then the approval came through for its use as a treatment for SAD. Now that it was legal to do so, in 2000 Glaxo spent $91.7 million advertising Paxil for that disorder. In April 2001, the drug got additional approval as a treatment for generalized anxiety disorder. In the first half of the following year, Glaxo spent another $60 million promoting it. Glaxo now has approval to sell another form of the drug, Paxil CR, one advantage of which is that it is not absorbed in the stomach but in the small intestine, resulting in fewer side effects than with the regular form. From the point of view of a drug company, it's simple: more FDA approvals, more ability to legally advertise, more sales. Glaxo even hired as a spokesman Ricky Williams, the recently retired Miami Dolphins running back who suffers from social anxiety and takes Paxil to treat it. This, too, undoubtedly helped sales. But knowing all this doesn't change the most important fact: Paxil works.

Paxil comes in 10 mg, 20 mg, and 30 mg pills as well as in a liquid form and in controlled release pills of 12.5 mg, 25 mg, and 37.5 mg. It has various side effects, including sweating, nausea, dry mouth, constipation, decreased appetite, somnolence, tremor, decreased libido, yawning, abnormal ejaculation, inability to achieve orgasm, and impotence. This is a substantial list of side effects, and probably most patients will suffer at least one of them. But, as with the other SSRIs whose side effects are similar, they often disappear as drug therapy progresses. There has been recent controversy about the use of Paxil in children with depression, since some studies suggest that a small percentage of children with depression using the drug may experience hostility or suicidal ideas. It is also possible that this small subgroup may have undetected bipolar illness and experience an exacerbation while using the drug. Children with depression or anxiety disorders should always be screened for bipolar disorder before starting treatment. The FDA now requires that a special warning, called a black box, be added to the indications for all antidepressants (including those not chemically related to the SSRIs), stating that there may be a risk of suicide when the medicine is used in children and adolescents. Paxil CR may have fewer side effects than the original Paxil—less nausea, and perhaps less weight gain and sexual side effects.

❖ START LOW, GO SLOW

Ever since childhood, the young man in my office told me, he had suffered from what were obviously the symptoms of social anxiety disorder. He was always shy, the kind of toddler who hid behind his mother's legs whenever an unfamiliar person approached. He'd started out in a parochial school, where his parents thought he would feel more comfortable, but rather than opening up and making friends, his shyness and ensuing loneliness only seemed to grow worse. He then transferred to the public elementary school because his parents felt he "needed to meet a wider range of people." They were well aware of their son's problems and were trying (though without professional help) to do the right thing for him. It didn't work. He went through elementary school, high school, and three years of college, suffering almost all the time. He was reluctant to speak in class, terrified at the idea of asking a girl for a date, and generally avoided contact with others. When he dropped out of college just before the end of his junior year, he took a job as a clerk working for the New York City Transit Authority, spending his day photocopying papers and hiding in his cubicle. He spent his evenings in his studio apartment alone. When I met this twenty-four-year-old African-American, it didn't take long to figure out that in addition to his social anxiety, he was seriously depressed and, judging from his story, had probably suffered from both these disorders for a long time. He was in psychotherapy with a social worker (whom I know and whose skills I very much respect), which he found helpful and interesting, but his symptoms were still paralyzing. I started him on Paxil CR at 12.5 mg for a week, increasing it to 25 mg. As with other SSRIs, it can take as long as eight weeks for the pills to work well, and the more you take at the beginning, the more likely you are to feel side effects. "Start low, go slow" is usually the best approach with all psychotropic medicines. So going to 25 mg after a week was fairly aggressive—it's normal to wait as long as eight weeks before raising the dosage that much—but in this case there were no side effects at all, so an aggressive approach seemed warranted. Initially, I had him take the dose in the morning, but it made him drowsy, so we switched to an evening dose. After three weeks there was a general improvement in his mood and level of optimism. Then, one week after that, he had substantial reduction of anxiety in most social situations—he started engaging people in his office, going on dates, even going on a job interview. This last, he felt, was the biggest breakthrough—he and everyone else knew that the job he had was beneath his talents. He continued on 25 mg at bedtime, and he's continuing to make progress in facing his fears. In addition, many of the negative cognitions associated with these social situations have dissipated.

ZOLOFT

The generic name of Zoloft is sertraline. It was the second drug approved by the FDA for the treatment of social anxiety disorder, and it is also used to treat a number of other psychiatric disorders, including major depression, obsessive-compulsive disorder, panic disorder, and premenstrual dysphoric disorder. In one study about half of people with social anxiety who took Zoloft felt better, as opposed to about a quarter who felt better with a placebo (sugar pill), a statistically significant difference. There wasn't enough data on race and age to see if these factors made a difference, but gender did not.

Then researchers did a long-term study to see whether those who responded well to the drug would relapse if the drug were stopped. Using a placebo for half the group of responders after 24 weeks of therapy, they demonstrated that those who continued the drug relapsed less frequently than those who stopped it.

Like all of the drugs discussed here, Zoloft has side effects, which vary considerably in kind and intensity from patient to patient. For example, Zoloft can cause sleepiness in some people and insomnia in others. Other common side effects are dry mouth, diarrhea, and nausea. It can also cause delayed ejaculation in some men.

Zoloft is sold in tablets of 25 mg, 50 mg, and 100 mg, which are scored so that they can be easily split in half. It is also available in a liquid form. The usual starting dose is 25 mg, which can be increased to up to 200 mg a day.

❖ TREATING TWO DISORDERS AT ONCE

I treated a forty-year-old woman executive who worked for a large reinsurance company. I've never understood exactly what a reinsurance company does, but suffice it to say that she had a high-level and high-paying position, and her work entailed the supervision of a number of other employees. Mira had worked for the same company since graduating from business school and had risen in rank and salary despite her long-term social anxiety symptoms. She wasn't married and generally led a solitary life, but she viewed this as a kind of sacrifice demanded by the challenging career she'd chosen. Thus she didn't come to see me because of her social anxiety—she was succeeding in her work despite it, and though she was aware of her problem she had learned to live with it. "Everyone has problems at work," she told me. "Mine are no worse than anyone's." But something else had now happened that compelled her to seek psychiatric care: she had been sexually assaulted about three months before she came to see me. After the attack, she developed all the symptoms of post-traumatic stress disorder. Superimposed on her original social anxiety, this additional pain was finally too great even for a person of her obvious emotional strength. I gave her 25 mg of Zoloft in the morning, which gave her some transient nausea and made her feel jittery. After three weeks, these side effects disappeared, and we raised the dose to 50 mg in the morning. Her mood improved significantly, she saw a decrease in intrusive flashbacks about the rape, experienced less of a startle reaction, and felt more like herself. She also found it easier to interact with people at work and in other social relationships, and said that for the first time the sense of dread that she had on facing many work-related social situations was dramatically reduced. From the way Mira described it, it seemed as if she viewed the mitigation of her social anxiety symptoms as a kind of happy side benefit of the treatment!

EFFEXOR

Effexor (the generic name is venlafaxine) was approved by the FDA in early 2003 for the treatment of social anxiety disorder. It is also approved for treating depression and generalized anxiety disorder, obsessive compulsive disorder, panic disorder, and post-traumatic stress disorder. Psychiatrists have been using it successfully for some time for SAD.

Effexor inhibits the reuptake of both serotonin and norepinephrine, and is therefore strictly speaking an SNRI—a serotonin-norepinephrine reuptake inhibitor. Effexor, for similar reasons as Paxil, is not approved for children under eighteen. In addition to the usual side effects—sleepiness, wakefulness, nausea—Effexor can cause elevated blood pressure at higher doses in a small percentage of susceptible people.

Effexor also comes as Effexor XR, an extended release form with fewer side effects for some people, including less nausea and less blood pressure elevation. In almost all cases, I prescribe the XR, which comes in 37.5 mg, 75 mg, and 150 mg tablets.

Effexor comes in 25 mg, 37.5 mg, 50 mg, 75 mg, and 100 mg tablets. The usual dose starts at 75 mg and can be increased gradually

❖ HAVING IT ALL

Some people seem to have it all: major depression, generalized anxiety disorder, social anxiety disorder, and obsessive-compulsive disorder—all in one pain-wracked person. I had such a person in my practice, a thirty-seven-year-old married woman who had been at home taking care of her daughter since her birth nine years before. As Anne's daughter required less and less parental attention, her own symptoms grew worse. Anne was sad most of the day, especially on waking. She was picking up what are practically textbook obsessive-compulsive habits—wiping her kitchen counter again and again, even when it hadn't been used, checking the locks on her door twice every time she left home, twisting her hair compulsively. And she was isolated. When her daughter was younger, she had a circle of acquaintances— "playground pals," as she called them, because the only time she ever saw them was at the playground—but none of these connections was strong enough to persist as their kids grew older. Anne was disinclined to seek out new friends. She was, in short, miserable. She'd been in psychotherapy for some months, and she found it useful and wanted to continue. But her symptoms weren't going away. I prescribed 37.5 mg Effexor XR for a week, and, since she had no side effects, we raised the dose to 75 mg. After two weeks, there was significant improvement in her social anxiety symptoms, but she continued to have some depressive symptoms and the obsessive-compulsive behavior wasn't getting better. I then raised the dose to 150 mg a day for two weeks, then went up to 225 mg a day. There was a complete remission of the depression and substantial reduction in the obsessive-compulsive symptoms, in addition to less anxiety in social situations. Finally, on this dose Anne had more interest in engaging in various kinds of activities—taking night classes, starting an exercise regimen, calling old friends. She felt that for the first time she was really back at a normal level of participation in social and community activities.

to about 225 mg until the desired effect is achieved. In severe cases of depression, doses of up to 375 mg per day can be used.

Other Serotonin Reuptake Inhibitors Used in SAD

FLUVOXAMINE

This drug, one of the older SSRIs, used to be sold under the brand name Luvox and is now available only as a generic. Its primary use and its only current indication is in treating obsessive-compulsive disorder both in adults and children. The typical dosage is 100 mg to 300 mg a day, with a starting dose of 50 mg. There is an economic advantage: because it's a generic, it's cheaper than drugs that are sold by only one company. At least one study supports the use of fluvoxamine for children who suffer from SAD, but the study's findings concerning extended treatment of pediatric anxiety disorders are only preliminary, since the study was uncontrolled.

PROZAC

Prozac was the first SSRI and is now available in a generic form (fluoxetine) at a fraction of the cost of the brand name drug. Although there are vastly different reactions in different people, fluoxetine has a long usage history—it was first introduced to the U.S. market in 1988, and quickly became one of the most prescribed medicines in the country. Millions of people have taken it. It is generally well tolerated when used over long periods of time, and it differs from other SSRIs in that it has a much longer half-life—it stays in the body for weeks after you stop taking it. This has advantages: if you miss some doses, or just suddenly stop taking it, you don't experience the uncomfortable withdrawal symptoms that can result when you stop taking other drugs. Lilly, the original manufacturer, still sells Prozac under the brand name and under the name Sarafem for the treatment of premenstrual dysphoric disorder. Prozac is chemically identical to the generic forms of the drug, although there may be small differences in the way the body metabolizes the ingredients. Lilly also sells a once-a-week version of the medicine called Prozac Weekly. Fluoxetine is available in 10 mg and 20 mg pills, 40 mg capsules, and in a liquid form.

Even though fluoxetine is used successfully in the treatment of social anxiety disorder, the scientific evidence for its effectiveness is mixed. In one pilot study testing the drug with people suffering from SAD, the drug was found no more effective than a placebo, and yet in other studies it has been found to be significantly more effective. Results from one study suggest that some people who don't respond to fluvoxamine may respond to fluoxetine.

❖ A GIFTED YOUNG ATHLETE

I treated a ten-year-old boy named Adam who was a good student and a remarkable athlete. He played shortstop for his Little League team, and his father, a former college tennis player, had taught him to play tennis well enough to keep up with teenaged opponents, if not actually beat them. On the field, or on the court, he looked like a kid who was totally self-possessed, completely in control of himself. There was no way to tell from watching Adam with a baseball bat or a tennis racket in his hands that he had terrible separation anxiety and social anxiety, so paralyzing that it kept him out of school for as much as three weeks every semester. Terrified of leaving his parents, terrified of being called on in class, terrified of socializing with other kids, this gifted young athlete looked entirely different when he wasn't engaging in sports. His parents were well aware of his problems, and he'd had several sessions of psychotherapy with a very good child psychiatrist. But he wasn't especially fond of talking about himself, and he and the psychiatrist agreed that something more was needed. I gave him 25 mg of Luvox at bedtime, raising it to 50 mg for a week, then to 100 mg for two weeks, and finally 150 mg. Initial nausea and sedation side effects disappeared, and after four weeks Adam felt that it was easier for him to separate from his family and go to school in the morning. He also had less persistent fear about being called on in class.

CELEXA

Celexa (generic name citalopram) had been used in more than 8 million patients in other countries before the FDA approved it for treating depression in 1998. It is also used, although much less often, for treating anxiety disorders, including SAD. Celexa can cause the usual SSRI side effects—nausea, sleep problems, appetite disruptions, dry mouth, dizziness, and sexual problems. Celexa is usually started at 20 mg per day and can go as high as 40 mg, increased gradually over at least one week. Doses higher than 40 mg don't produce better results. It comes in 10 mg, 20 mg, and 40 mg pills, and in a liquid form, and the 20 mg and 40 mg tablets are scored so you can break them in half easily. There have been no large trials of citalopram in patients with social anxiety, although there have been a number of smaller studies.

Lexapro

Escitalopram is the generic name for Lexapro, and it is a derivative of the same chemical as Celexa. As of this writing, it is the newest SSRI, and it is approved for treating major depression. Studies suggest that it may be more effective than citalopram in treating both depression and anxiety disorders. It scores well in side effects, too. In some studies, the same number of people discontinue Lexapro because of side effects as those who discontinue a placebo because of side effects. It should be emphasized that there have been so far no large placebo-controlled randomized studies of the drug to treat social anxiety, but preliminary findings strongly suggest that it is, like the other SSRIs, quite effective.

It can take about a month for the drug to have its effect—as with the other SSRIs, it's worth sticking to the program for several weeks before giving up. Nausea, insomnia, and ejaculation disorders are the most common side effects, and the side effects increase as the dose is raised from 10 mg a day to 20 mg. Decreased libido is more common in men than in women taking Lexapro. Dosage is between 10 mg and 20 mg a day, and the drug is supplied in 10 mg and 20 mg scored pills. The dosage should start at 10 mg and not be increased for at least a week. There isn't any benefit in raising the dose above 20 mg.

I recently treated a thirty-year-old woman with panic disorder and SAD by giving 10 mg of Lexapro in the morning. She had some nausea, but it passed. After three weeks, there was a significant reduction in the frequency and severity of panic attacks, and much less anticipatory anxiety at entering social situations.

Serotonin Antagonists

The two drugs that fit into this category of serotonin antagonists affect the chemicals produced at the nerve endings, but do so in slightly different ways from either SSRIs or SNRIs, and are chemically unrelated to those drugs. SSRIs and SNRIs function by blocking the clearance or reuptake of neurotransmitters (serotonin and norepinephrine, respectively) from the synaptic cleft (the tiny space in between nerve cells), thus allowing for more neurotransmitters to stimulate the receptors. Serotonin antagonists, on the other hand, chemically bind to the neurotransmitter receptor, blocking the effect of the neurotransmitters. Different process, similar result.

SERZONE

The generic name is nefazodone, and it has FDA approval only as an antidepressant. Even though there are limited scientific studies of its usefulness in treating social anxiety, those studies suggest that it can work in some patients, at least for the generalized form of the disorder.

The worst side effect of this drug is that it can cause liver problems, so people with any kind of liver dysfunction shouldn't use it, and those who do use it should be alert to any symptoms of liver disorder (jaundice, gastrointestinal pains, loss of appetite, and so on). Because of this, it is infrequently used. There have been rare reports of priapism—prolonged and inappropriate erections—and if this occurs, the drug should be stopped immediately and the physician should be consulted. In premarket clinical trials that involved more than three thousand patients, about 16 percent went off the drug because of side effects, the most common of which were nausea, dizziness, insomnia, a general feeling of weakness, and agitation.

Serzone is usually started at 200 mg a day divided into two doses, then increased gradually. The effective dose is usually between 300 mg and 600 mg, split into two doses per day. The drug is supplied in 50 mg, 100 mg, 150 mg, 200 mg, and 250 mg pills. The 100 mg and the 150 mg pills are scored so you can split them in half.

The exact mechanism of action, as with the other drugs described here, is not really known, but it predominantly blocks post-synaptic serotonin receptors. The drug is safe with careful use, and although it would probably not be the first choice for social anxiety disorder, it can work in patients who don't get better on other drugs.

TRAZODONE

Trazodone, the other serotonin antagonist, used to be sold under the brand name Deseryl but is now available only as a generic. The drug is approved only for treating depression, and even though there are few scientific studies supporting its effectiveness in treating SAD, it can be and has been used in treating this disorder as well. Trazodone is often given in small doses to help people sleep. Priapism with Trazodone is an even greater risk than it is with Serzone, and many doctors, including me, do not prescribe it for men for this reason. However, it may be used in men at low doses as a sleeping aid.

Monoamine Oxidase Inhibitors

Monoamine oxidase inhibitors, sometimes referred to as MAO inhibitors or MAOIs, are a group of closely related antidepressants that have been in use much longer than the SSRIs, although now the

SSRIs have largely replaced them in treating depression. These include Nardil (phenelzine), Parnate (tranylcypromine), Eldepryl (selegiline), and Marplan (isocarboxazid).

One of the big problems with these drugs is that they require strict dietary restrictions. People who take them can get dangerously high blood pressure if they eat food that contains an amino acid called tyramine, which means eliminating, among other foods, most things that have been aged, smoked, or fermented. This requires a total ban on a number of foods that many people find delicious: pickled herring, smoked fish, beer, wine, liver, yeast extract (including brewer's yeast in large quantities), dry sausage (including Genoa salami, hard salami, pepperoni, and Lebanon bologna), pods of broad beans (fava beans), many cheeses, and yogurt. Large amounts of chocolate and caffeine can also cause problems. Despite these drawbacks, MAO inhibitors have been found effective in treating social anxiety.

NARDIL

Phenelzine is the chemical name. Nardil has been proven useful in depressed patients who also have anxieties and phobias. Given these facts, it was natural to try to use it with social anxiety disorder, and, while it would not be my first choice (mostly because of the dietary restrictions and other side effects), it is extremely effective in treating social anxiety. In fact, several very good placebo-controlled studies demonstrate that socially anxious patients respond more favorably to phenelzine than to cognitive behavioral therapy. Normally, the drug is started at 15 mg a day, and then increased gradually up to 60 mg over the course of a month. If there is no response at this point, and if the side effects are absent or at least tolerable, the dose can be gradually increased to as high as 90 mg a day. It is supplied in a 15 mg tablet.

PARNATE

Its chemical name is tranylcypromine, and it is approved for the treatment of major depression. But its use in social anxiety disorder has not been as widely studied as that of Nardil. There is some evidence that it works, but there are no carefully controlled studies of the drug, so its use in the treatment of social anxiety is still scientifically questionable. Tablets containing 10 mg of the drug are sold, and the dosage is usually 30 mg a day divided into three doses.

Reversible Inhibitors of Monoamine Oxidase

In an attempt to overcome the dietary problems of the irreversible MAO inhibitors, researchers developed several reversible inhibitors of monoamine oxidase (RIMAs) that have similar therapeutic effects while minimizing the dietary restrictions. Neither of these two drugs is presently available for sale in the United States, but studies have been undertaken to test their effectiveness.

MOCLOBEMIDE

The brand name is Manerix, and the drug inhibits the reuptake of serotonin, norepinephrine, and dopamine. This means increased concentrations of these neurotransmitters, which probably account for it therapeutic effect. The effect lasts a short time, usually 24 hours or less.

Researchers have studied the drug when taken with tyramine, and findings suggest that problems can be avoided if the drug is given after, instead of before, consuming tyramine-rich foods. That's the good news for social anxiety sufferers. The bad news is that studies have shown that the drug relieves symptoms in only a minority of patients, usually only slightly more than those who experience relief on a placebo.

BROFAROMINE

Brofaromine is sold under the brand name Consonar. It is closely related to moclobemide, and it blocks the metabolism (or break-down) of serotonin, norepinephrine, and dopamine. There have been three placebo-controlled studies of the drug, and brofaromine has been found much more effective than moclobemide. It works (at least in these studies) with about three-quarters of socially anxious patients who take it, a rate much better than the placebo.

Benzodiazepines

A number of drugs fit into this chemical group, and the most famil-iar one (although it is not used for social anxiety) is Valium. Klonopin (clonazepam), Xanax (alprazolam), and Broman (bromazepam) are all benzodiazepines that have been studied and used for the treat-ment of social anxiety. Klonopin in particular has been shown to be effective. While these drugs have good results with some patients, there may be serious problems associated with them, including the possibility of physical dependence and withdrawal symptoms. In addition, the number of studies on using them for social anxiety dis-order is quite limited. Few psychiatrists would prescribe benzodi-azepines as a first-line treatment for social anxiety. The drugs are used for people who don't respond to other treatment, or to get some immediate relief while starting an SSRI. The benzodiazepine is tapered as the SSRI begins to work.

XANAX

The generic name of Xanax is alprazolam. It is FDA approved for the treatment of generalized anxiety disorder and panic disorder. However, a double-blind study of the drug for treating social anxi-ety revealed that it was not terribly effective—only about a third of patients responded well to it. The maximum dose for treating generalized anxiety disorder is 4 mg per day, but for panic disorder, doses as high as 10 mg a day have been effective. It comes in .25 mg, .5 mg, 1 mg, and 2 mg scored pills. Xanax has a form called Xanax XR, a once-a-day formulation that may be associated with less rebound anxiety and fewer withdrawal symptoms when it is stopped.

Klonopin

Klonopin (clonazepam) has FDA approval for the treatment of seizure disorders and panic disorder. Although doses higher than the normal 1 mg per day sometimes produce more side effects, nevertheless doses up to 4 mg have been used successfully in the treatment of social anxiety. Somnolence, dizziness, nervousness, and depression are the most common side effects. It comes in .5 mg, 1 mg, and 2 mg pills.

Bromazepam

Bromazepam is sold under the brand name Lectopam in Canada, but it is not sold in the United States. Studies have shown it to be significantly more effective than a placebo, with a response rate approaching 85 percent. As with the other benzodiazepines, the side effects of dependency and withdrawal symptoms make this drug difficult to use.

Beta-Adrenergic Blockers

There is some anecdotal evidence, though no scientific proof, that beta-blockers, drugs used mainly to treat cardiovascular problems, might be helpful in treating certain kinds of social anxiety. In one study, however, atenolol (brand name Tenormin), one of the beta-blocking drugs, was found to be inferior to behavioral treatments.

Beta-blockers shouldn't be used with people who have diabetes, asthma, or some heart diseases, but they usually have few side effects in otherwise healthy people. Propanolol (Inderal is the brand name) is another beta-blocker that may be useful for discrete problems such as performance anxiety or stage fright. Beta-blockers have no effect for the generalized type of social anxiety.

I often treat patients with discrete performance anxiety—public speakers or musicians, for example, with beta-blockers. I will prescribe 25 to 50 mg of atanolol or 10 to 20 mg of propanolol one hour before a performance situation. Patients can have a dramatic decrease in sweating, tremors, rapid heart rate, and palpitations, and thus enable them to perform confidently.

Other Drugs

There are drugs that are used rarely in treating social anxiety disorder, usually when other drugs and psychotherapy have proved ineffective. I'll briefly describe them here, but generally they are used for SAD only in scientific studies.

BUSPIRONE

This is sold under the brand name BuSpar and is available as a generic as well. It is indicated for anxiety, but studies have shown that using it alone for social anxiety or performance anxiety is ineffective. It may help as an additive treatment for people taking SSRIs who are not responding well to them. Sometimes BuSpar can help with preventing side effects of SSRIs.

NEURONTIN

Gabapentin is the chemical name for this drug, and it is FDA approved as a treatment for epileptic seizures. At least one study has demonstrated that high doses of Neurontin can be effective in treating social anxiety. Even though only a minority of patients responded well to the drug, the number was significantly greater than the number responding to placebo.

TOFRANIL

Imipramine was sold under the brand name Tofranil but is now available as a generic. It is a tricyclic antidepressant, the group of antidepressants that were the first-line treatment for major depression before the introduction of the SSRIs. It has been used successfully in the treatment of school phobia in children, and there is some weak evidence for its effectiveness in treating other phobias, though when studied for social anxiety it proved ineffective.

CLOMIPRAMINE

Clomipramine (Anafranil) is another tricyclic indicated for depression and obsessive-compulsive disorder, but it would not normally be used for social anxiety alone.

CLONIDINE

Sold under the brand name Catapres as an anti-hypertension drug, clonidine has been little studied in treating social anxiety. What studies there are show it to be generally ineffective.

WELLBUTRIN

Wellbutrin (bupropion) is an antidepressant that is chemically unrelated to other antidepressant medicines. It inhibits the reuptake dopamine and to some extent norepinephrine. Its use in social anxiety is limited, and it has not been widely studied for this indication, but there is some evidence that it might work for some patients. At least one recent study using the sustained-release version of the drug showed some beneficial effects.

A physician has a wide choice of drugs for the treatment of social anxiety, but it should be remembered that drug treatment in combination with psychological treatment is almost always more effective than drug treatment alone. It is also generally true that drugs often stop working after you stop taking them, while psychological treatments can have more lasting effects in preventing relapse. These drugs are not aspirin—you can't "take two and call me in the morning." They require constant attention from a skilled practitioner, adjusting doses, adding or changing medicines, trying different drugs until the right medicine and the right dosage are found. Because most of them take a long time to start working, and because side effects can be troubling, they also require persistence and dedication on the part of the patient. Yet there is ample evidence that a person with social anxiety who is taking the right drug in the right dosage can experience relief so profound that it can be life-changing.

Making Your Own Contribution to Clinical Research

Research on the effectiveness of medical treatments depends on clinical trials, and clinical trials depend on volunteers. This is just as true for studies of social anxiety disorder as for any other health problem. Participating in such trials entails risks and benefits that anyone suffering from social anxiety should know about.

A clinical trial is research that uses volunteers as human subjects to help answer a given scientific question. Does paroxetine work better than fluoxetine for social anxiety disorder? Will there be fewer relapses among people treated with cognitive therapy than among those treated with Zoloft? Does St. John's wort have an effect greater than a placebo in helping people who suffer from SAD? Such questions can only be answered definitively through large-scale testing with human volunteers.

There are various kinds of clinical trials, each with a different aim:

- **Treatment trials** test new drugs or treatment procedures.
- **Prevention trials** test ways to prevent disease or relapse in people who have already had a disease.

- **Diagnostic trials** seek better methods of diagnosing illnesses.
- **Screening trials** test ways of detecting disease.
- **Quality-of-life trials** examine methods for helping and comforting those with chronic illnesses.

No matter what the type of clinical trial, the procedure is more or less the same. Usually (although not always, as we will see), a number of volunteers of a statistically significant size is divided into two groups, one to receive the treatment under consideration, the other, called the control group, to receive either a placebo or the standard treatment for the disorder. The groups are matched for age, sex, general health, and a number of other criteria to be sure that they are equivalent. Except that the control group does not actually receive the medicine or procedure under test, it is treated in exactly the same way as the group that receives the actual treatment. They are given sugar pills or dummy procedures, and in double-blind studies neither the researchers conducting the experiment nor the participants know which group they are in. This method prevents the possibility that a person, knowing that he is being given a new treatment, might expect it to work better and therefore report improvement where there really isn't any. It also prevents the researcher, eager for positive results, from seeing improvement where objectively there is none. Only researchers who are not involved in day-to-day clinical care of the patients know which patient is in which group, information they will keep to themselves until the study ends or until a medical reason arises to reveal it before the study ends. The treatment proceeds for a predetermined amount of time, and then the results are evaluated to see if the treatment group did better than the placebo group.

These trials are usually the idea of a researcher who receives a grant to carry out a study. The grants come from private foundations or government agencies such as the National Institutes of Health, the Department of Defense, or the National Institute of Mental Health. Often studies of new drugs are paid for by pharmaceutical companies, which raises other concerns, which we will get to in a moment.

Studies of new drugs and treatment are divided into four phases. Phase I trials test a small number of people, usually a few dozen or less, with a drug or treatment that has never been used on humans before. This is the first evaluation of safety, safe dosage range, and side effects. If this goes well, in Phase II the drug is given to a larger group of people, usually several hundred, to further test its effects and safety. After its successful completion, Phase III begins, in which the drug is given to several thousand people to test its efficacy and to collect a sufficient amount of information to have a statistically significant number of participants from which to draw conclusions. Finally, Phase IV begins after a drug is marketed to study its side effects in a large population and to determine the best ways to use it.

How Subjects Are Chosen

Figuring out who is an acceptable subject requires the consideration of various criteria. Age, gender, the type or severity of disease, the previous treatment history, and the general health of the potential participant are all considered. Some studies need participants with particular illnesses; some need healthy people; some need both. If you meet the "inclusion criteria" and are not disallowed by meeting one of the "exclusion criteria," then you can be a subject in the study.

Some exceptions are made for people suffering from a life-threatening or serious disease for which there is no good alternative treatment. Such people would be allowed into a study even if they did not meet the normal criteria for inclusion, provided the treatment they are being considered for is actively being researched in controlled studies and there is evidence that they might be helped by the treatment. Such a situation would rarely, if ever, apply in clinical trials of psychotropic medicines.

❖ WHO'S IN AND WHO'S OUT: INCLUSION AND EXCLUSION CRITERIA

Here's a typical listing of inclusion and exclusion criteria, taken from the website www.clinicaltrials.gov, a useful source for finding out about studies recruiting subjects in your geographical area. This listing is for a study comparing cognitive behavioral therapy and paroxetine (Paxil) in the treatment of social anxiety disorder.

Ages Eligible for Study: 18 Years–65 Years
Genders Eligible for Study: Both Criteria

Inclusion Criteria:
- DSM-IV criteria for generalized social phobia
- Willing and able to give written informed consent
- English-speaking

Exclusion Criteria:
- Prior or current diagnosis of schizophrenia, schizoaffective disorder, organic mental disorder, bipolar disorder, or antisocial, schizotypal, and schizoid personality disorders
- Suicidal thoughts
- History of failed paroxetine treatment of at least 6 weeks' duration at adequate doses or a history of failed outcome of a previous adequate trial of CBT [cognitive behavior therapy].
- Clinically significant and/or unstable medical disease

- Pregnancy or breast-feeding. Women of childbearing potential will be required to sign a statement indicating their intention to avoid pregnancy during the study through the use of an effective method of contraception.
- Alcohol or substance abuse or dependence within the past 3 months. Patients with a positive drug screen but no substance abuse disorder will be eligible for the study, provided they have not met criteria for abuse/dependence within the last 6 months and provide two clean urine samples 2 weeks apart.
- Current or past history of seizure disorder (except febrile seizure in childhood)
- Conditions that contraindicate the use of paroxetine
- Inability to tolerate or unwillingness to accept a drug-free period of 4 weeks for monoamine oxidase inhibitors (MAOIs) or fluoxetine and 2 weeks for other selective serotonin reuptake inhibitors (SSRIs), neuroleptics, antidepressants, benzodiazepines, mood stabilizers, buspirone, beta-adrenergic blockers, or other psychotropic drugs prior to beginning the study
- Currently receiving psychotherapy

Volunteering for a Study: Pro and Con

If you volunteer for a clinical trial you may gain access to new research treatments before they are widely available. You may obtain medical care from leading experts in the field while the trial goes on, usually at no charge, and you will have the satisfaction of involving yourself personally in important medical research. Even though all the risks of a given experimental treatment are not known (if they were, there would be considerably less need for the research), investigational treatments are carefully tested for safety before being used in a clinical trial. If a patient becomes ill during a trial, even if the illness is not due to the treatment, he will be removed from the study and immediately be given medical care. You will be told the results of the research, and what the results mean for you in particular. The results may not be in for a long time—studies can run for several years before there are any publishable findings—but you will get the results when they are ready.

There are drawbacks as well. First, any treatment can involve side effects, some of which can be serious or even life-threatening. Being in a trial may require a considerable commitment of time and effort that not all people are willing to make. You may have to travel to treatment sites, fill out lengthy questionnaires, follow complex dosing schedules, and be available at specific times for examination. Hospital stays may sometimes be required. It may be that the research requires that a certain drug be administered in a specific dose or in a specific way (by injection, say) that may or may not be exactly right for you, and it may be impossible to adjust the dose during the clinical trial. You may find yourself in a control group that receives no treatment at all. And finally, even if you are in the treatment group, even if you conscientiously devote the required energy and time to the project, and even if you follow all the rules, the treatment itself may fail, leaving you with the feeling that you have accomplished little—even though in fact you have made a significant contribution to the progress of treatment research and are to be congratulated for your courage and unselfish devotion.

Enrolling in a Trial

Clinical trials with human subjects are carefully regulated. Researchers must report their results at scientific conferences, in journals, and, if the research is funded by the government, to the funding agency. Every institution carrying on research must by law have an Institutional Review Board (IRB) made up of independent experts, including physicians, other scientists and researchers, and members of the public who approve the initial protocol (the plan on which the trial is based) and periodically review the research to make sure that it is being carried out correctly. You may read this protocol, and you can even ask for a copy of it to take home and discuss with your family, your friends, or your physician. Before you enter a clinical trial, you must read and sign an informed consent document which outlines the aims of the study, its procedures, its duration, and its possible risks and benefits. This document is not a contract, and you can withdraw from a trial at any time you wish, for any reason or for no reason. Signing the informed consent document is not the end of the process—during the study you must be provided with continuing information about any new risks discovered during the course of the investigation, and the researchers conducting the study must respond satisfactorily to any questions you may have about them.

Questions to Ask

Even before enrolling, you should be prepared to ask and get complete answers to a range of questions. The purpose of the study should be clear to you. You should also ask if the new treatment has ever been used before and what evidence there is for its effectiveness.

If you are under a conventional treatment, you should clarify why the researchers believe that this new treatment might be better for you. The length of the trial and the amount of time you will have to commit to it should be specified from the outset. Whether you will

---

❖ INFORMED CONSENT

The informed consent document is not an informal or free-hand description of the research being undertaken. Although it is written in a way that people without medical or scientific training can understand, it is nevertheless a formal document that can be lengthy and complex. It must contain, at least, these eight basic parts:

1. A statement that the study involves research and that describes the goals, methods, and length of time the study will involve.
2. A description of the risks or discomforts that you might experience during the research.
3. A description of the benefits the treatment may yield, to you and others.
4. A statement of the alternative courses of treatment that might help you.
5. A description of how your privacy will be protected.
6. A description of compensation or medical treatments that will be available if the research causes harm to your health.
7. The name of the person to contact about your rights, and the name of the person to contact about injury or illness.
8. A statement that the research is voluntary and that you may withdraw from it at any time without jeopardizing any of your other rights under the agreement.

be reimbursed for expenses should be discussed—if you will have to travel long distances—or even short distances, for that matter—who is going to pay the carfare? Who is paying for the treatment, and what kinds of treatment are covered? You will want to know if the trial involves hospitalization, and if so, when and for how long? The kind of follow-up care you will receive after the trial ends should also be discussed. You will want to know who is providing your care and how they are qualified to do so. And you will want to be assured that your normal health care provider is involved in the process to assure that whatever treatments you are currently receiving are not interfered with by your participation in the clinical trial.

Compassionate Plea

Suppose the treatment under study works well for you. Are you then entitled to continue using the drug or treatment even though it is experimental? The answer is usually yes. If the drug under consideration has already been approved for use by the FDA and is in use for another indication, your own doctor can prescribe the drug for your problem. If the drug has not yet been approved by the FDA but has obvious benefits for you, you can get permission to use it under what is called a compassionate plea basis. Using this approach, the manufacturer of the drug can give the drug to your doctor, who can then prescribe it for you. But there are some circumstances under which you cannot continue to use the drug even though it helps you. If, for example, the manufacturer is not ready to release the drug before further investigation even under the compassionate plea system, he is not obliged to do so—the manufacturer might be especially concerned if prescribing the drug requires special knowledge on the part of the physician. Or the manufacturer may have produced only a small amount of the drug, sufficient for the clinical trial but not enough to prescribe to all for whom it works. The issue of compassionate plea use of the treatment under study should be brought up with the investigators before you agree to participate in the trial.

Who Pays for Testing Drugs? Who Benefits?

Testing new drugs for Food and Drug Administration (FDA) approval is, as we mentioned in chapter 9 on pharmacological treatments, an expensive proposition. In our system, it is often drug companies, not independent government agencies, who pay for research on new medicines. In fact, drug companies spend more on researching drugs than the National Institutes of Health does in its grants to researchers. When scientists are granted research money from pharmaceutical companies, certain questions naturally arise about the objectivity of the work being done. After all, the company funding the research is hoping for positive results that will lead to FDA approval and then the marketing of the drug under consideration—if they didn't have this goal in mind, they wouldn't pay for the research. And drug companies do not like to see negative studies published of drugs they already have for sale. Everyone involved in pharmaceutical company–funded research—the researchers, the IRB (Institutional Review Board) that approves and supervises the research, the FDA to whom the studies will be submitted, and of course the drug companies themselves—knows that these things are true, and understands the risks to scientific objectivity that such arrangements may have. Therefore, making sure that the study is uninfluenced by monetary considerations is of paramount importance to everyone. Safeguards like randomization and double-blinding are in place to make sure that no bias influences the outcome of the study, but the issue is complex and controversial. We aren't going to settle the controversy in this book, but it is important to make some note of the problem.

Some argue that drug company–sponsored research inevitably produces more positive results than research sponsored by other sources, and that pharmaceutical companies actively discourage the publication of negative conclusions about their own drugs. If this is so, it may not mean that the studies funded by drug companies are necessarily flawed, but it may mean that other studies that should be published never see the light of day. In any case, this leaves many people uncomfortable.

An article published in the *British Journal of Psychiatry* concluded that when it comes to analyzing the costs of antidepressant medications, research sponsored by drug companies tends to conclude that their own newer SSRIs are more cost-effective than other older medicines, and that nonindustry-sponsored research articles, to a statistically significant degree, do not conclude they are cost-effective. What this means, however, is not so easy to say. The article drew no conclusions about the reasons for the discrepancy but only noted that it exists. In fact, the authors couldn't even draw any conclusions about which studies—the drug company–sponsored ones or the independently sponsored ones—were more accurate.

Any study must be read with a critical eye. This is true for government-funded studies as much as it is for studies funded by pharmaceutical companies. The fact is that for the foreseeable future in the United States, most research on new drugs, and on new uses for older drugs, will be carried on in the private sector—I know of no indication that the medical community is prepared to have it otherwise. Since that is the case, we are going to have to depend largely on the private financing of scientific studies in drug research, and we are going to have to deal with the questions that it raises. I optimistically believe that this can be done by following normal scientific procedures, without pointing fingers and without making accusations.

Studies Under Way Now

Right now, various studies are going on, and I'll describe a few below to give you an idea of the kinds of questions researchers are seeking to answer. By the time you read this, some information may be outdated, since clinical trials are an ongoing process. The best way to get current information on clinical trials is to check the website of the National Institutes of Health at www.clinicaltrials.gov. This site offers information on clinical trials in all fields of medicine, not just psychiatry. The studies that follow all concern trials on treatments for social anxiety:

Child/Adolescent Anxiety Multimodal Treatment Study. This is a study sponsored by the National Institute of Mental Health (NIMH) to compare two interventions for three different anxiety disorders: separation anxiety, social anxiety, and generalized anxiety disorder. The two treatments under study are Zoloft and cognitive behavioral therapy. It is a randomized, double-blind, placebo-controlled study in which otherwise healthy boys and girls 7 to 16 years old who have anxiety disorders are randomly assigned to receive Zoloft, cognitive behavioral therapy, a combination of the two, or a placebo. It will enroll 318 subjects, and as of this writing it is recruiting subjects. The study is large—it will take place at seven different sites in California, Maryland, New York, North Carolina, and Pennsylvania. And it will last a long time: it began in January 2003 and will not be completed until May 2007.

Treatment of Childhood Social Phobia. This is a randomized double-blind placebo-controlled study under the sponsorship of the NIMH. With a total enrollment of 250 children aged 8 to 16, the study will test Social Effectiveness Therapy for Children (SET-C) against fluoxetine (Prozac) and a placebo pill. The intent is to test the long-term effectiveness of these treatments, and so the study will last for four years, including a one-year follow-up to monitor the treatment's durability. The study is being carried out at the Maryland Center for Anxiety Disorders at the University of Maryland in College Park, Maryland. Subjects must have a diagnosis of social phobia to be included.

Social Phobia: Assessment and Treatment of Social Skills. Not all studies involve the use of drugs. This one compares two forms of behavioral treatment and measures them against a placebo treatment. The placebo in this case consists of being placed on a waiting list for treatment. The 16-week study will randomly assign adult men and women with a diagnosis of social phobia but who are otherwise healthy to one of three groups: an exposure therapy group, a social skills training and exposure group, or the waiting list control group. Using interviews, self-reports, and simulated role-playing, the researchers will assess the social skills of the participants before and after the treatment. The study, which will enroll 380 patients, will be undertaken at the University of Maryland in College Park, Maryland.

Generalized Anxiety Disorder and Social Anxiety Disorder: Their Impact on the Processing of Social Emotional Information and Instrumental Learning. This study has no randomization or control groups. Instead, it is an observational study that will look at the biological basis of generalized anxiety and social anxiety by investigating brain activity associated with specific thoughts and feelings. Subjects will be examined during three visits to the National Institutes of Health in Bethesda, Maryland. During the first visit, subjects will be asked questions about their general mood, degree of anxiety, their thinking skills, and behavior. They will then undergo a thorough physical exam including blood work, urinalysis, and an electrocardiogram. During a second visit, they will do various tasks while looking at a computer screen, tasks designed to lead them to experience specific kinds of thoughts and emotions. While they are doing these tasks, electrodes will be attached to their hands to monitor the electrical conductivity of the skin, a way of measuring muscle tension, one of the physical manifestations of anxiety. The third visit will be similar to the second, except that the tasks will be performed while the subject is lying in an MRI scanner. The study will include 60 adults between 20 and 65 years old. There will be patients who have no psychiatric diagnosis and patients with anxiety disorders, but the latter cannot be currently under treatment. Pregnant women are excluded because they cannot undergo MRI scans. Usually, study subjects are paid little or nothing, but in this one the participants are being paid up to $400.

St. John's Wort vs. Placebo in Social Phobia. There have been several studies that show that St. John's wort may be somewhat effective in treating mild to moderate depression. This study will investigate its effect on social anxiety. This is a 12-week, double-blind, and placebo-controlled study in which 40 patients will be assigned randomly to either the placebo group or a group that will receive a maximum of 1,800 mg a day of St. John's wort. Outcomes will be based on scores on the Liebowitz Social Anxiety Scale. The study is sponsored by the National Center for Complementary and Alternative Medicine, one of the centers of the National Institutes of Health. Patients of both sexes aged 18 to 65 are eligible, and the study is currently recruiting patients.

Participating in clinical trials is not for everyone. It requires considerable effort with no promise of significant reward, and a degree of altruism is required of anyone who decides to do this. But it is the only way for knowledge to be gained and for new treatments to be discovered. The more people who are willing to participate, the better for everyone. In pediatric oncology (cancer treatment for children), for example, every patient participates in some kind of trial or study, and as a result the field has progressed quickly—much more quickly than adult oncology, where participation in studies is not a requirement of treatment. Of course, psychiatric treatment requires no participation. But for some people participation can bring helpful new treatment, and others may receive less tangible but equally valuable rewards in knowing that they have made a significant contribution to the progress of clinical research. This kind of collaboration with scientists is something to be seriously considered when the opportunity arises.

Conclusion: Social Anxiety and the Brain—New Research

Social anxiety disorder, like other psychiatric disorders, has its origins in a malfunction of the brain, and it is in the brain itself that researchers are now looking to find answers about how these diseases affect us. Using new tools—magnetic resonance imaging, computerized axial tomography, positron emission tomography, magnetic resonance spectroscopy—and new drugs, researchers have discovered important information about the disorder. Neurobiological research of the causes of social anxiety is in its infancy, and practical clinical applications of current research are still far from clear, but much has already been learned.

If social anxiety originates in the brain, where in the brain is it? The question would have been impossible to answer, and may not even have been asked, just a few years ago. But now there are techniques, of which probably the most useful is functional magnetic resonance imaging (fMRI), that can actually locate thoughts and emotions in different parts of the brain. Why is this important for people with SAD?

MRI is probably at least vaguely familiar to most people as a kind of "super X ray" that can discern and produce detailed computerized pictures of human tissue. It works by detecting the small magnetic fields of hydrogen atoms. Since the human body is about 70 percent water, and since water molecules have two hydrogen atoms in each of them, that gives the machine quite a few tiny magnets to detect. But the magnetic field of a hydrogen atom is quite weak, and it requires a tremendously powerful magnet to detect it. An MRI machine is equipped with a magnet that is more than 50,000 times the strength of the earth's magnetic field and it has to be cooled to a temperature of 270 degrees below zero in order to work. (Don't try this at home.) When the tiny magnetic field of a hydrogen atom is exposed to such a powerful magnetic field, it aligns with it (the same way a compass needle aligns with the magnetic field of the earth). Then a pulse of radio-frequency energy is used to disturb the tiny magnets from their alignment. As the alignments return to normal, they give off tiny pulses of energy that can be detected by an antenna that surrounds the subject's body. This signal indicates the relative amounts of water molecules in different areas of tissue, and it can then be converted into a computerized picture of the tissue under examination. The brain, like the rest of the body, is mostly water, and different parts of the brain contain different amounts of water. Nerve cells, for example, have lots of water; fatty tissue has less. So detecting how water is distributed in the brain draws a detailed picture of differing kinds of brain tissue.

Functional MRI is an advanced MRI scanner that uses the same magnetic properties of the hydrogen atom to detect blood flow. Tissue near blood depleted of oxygen has different magnetic characteristics from those near freshly oxygenated blood, and fMRI can detect this difference to draw a picture of the brain in action. In using it on the human brain, researchers can trace the blood flow to various parts of the brain while various stimuli are shown to the subject. Although it takes a while sitting or lying down in a noisy machine in a position that can get uncomfortable, the procedure is, for all practical purposes, painless and harmless. The subject lies down with his head surrounded by a ring formed by the receiving coil. A high-resolution scan of the brain is made to provide the background against which the blood flow will be shown. Then a series of low-resolution scans are taken over a period of time—usually about 150 scans at 5-second intervals, which means this part of the procedure takes about 12 to 15 minutes. While these scans are going on, the patient is presented with various stimuli, often moving pictures, to trace the flow of blood to different parts of the brain as the patient watches the images. When the scan is finished, the set of images is analyzed. This involves applying various mathematical techniques and image-correcting tools to turn the images into three-dimensional pictures of the brain, with the blood flow highlighted as a different color overlaying the picture of the organ. Where the blood flows, activity is occurring, so you can, almost literally, watch a person thinking.

This technology opens many possibilities for investigators to watch the brain in action under various conditions, and there seems no limit to the phenomena that can be examined. Researchers have looked at a huge number of normal cognitive processes—memorization, the experience of pain, the recognition of faces, the taste of foods, and hundreds of others—and this has led to many insights about the ways the brain reacts to stimuli.

❧

Shy children, as we know, often grow into shy adults. Infants demonstrate this very early in life by their varying behavior: some love to approach novel or unfamiliar people or objects; others run and hide when faced with anything or anyone they haven't seen before. One study performed fMRI examinations on two groups of adults whose average age was about twenty-two: one group had, as two-year-olds, been characterized as very inhibited, the other as uninhibited. They presented both groups with pictures of novel and familiar faces. The adults who had been characterized as inhibited showed a greater response to novel faces than the uninhibited group in a particular part of the brain called the amygdala, demonstrating that this structure is in some way involved in this aspect of temperament. The research authors are careful to point out, however, that such amygdala activity is not necessarily diagnostic of social anxiety, and only two of the twenty-two subjects in this study suffered from the disorder. But the study did show how persistent temperament is from infancy through early adulthood, how much of it is "wired in" to our brains even before any environmental influences can have an impact. And it provided further evidence for the physical location of shyness in the brain.

The fMRI has also been used to study the injured or malfunctioning brain. The rehabilitation of stroke victims has been an area of particular interest, as has the study of the neurological basis for drug addiction, the dynamics of memory, and the progress of Alzheimer's disease, among many other phenomena. By watching the brain in action, it is now possible to see what areas of the brain are involved in various mental phenomena, knowledge that provides a novel angle of investigation for developing treatments for brain disorders. In addition to fMRI, several other imaging techniques are now in use. Computed tomography scan (CT scan) offers a detailed picture of the structures of the brain (though not its function). Positron emission tomography (PET scan) uses gamma-ray detectors to trace radioactively tagged oxygen, nitrogen, and other chemicals as they are metabolized in different areas of the brain. Angiography traces the blood vessels of the brain by following the route through the bloodstream of injected dye visible on X ray. For our purposes, the most pertinent use of the new imaging techniques is in the examination of the brains of people suffering from psychiatric illnesses, and particularly from social anxiety. Researchers are now beginning to get some ideas about what brain mechanisms are involved in the physiology of this mental disorder.

The PET scan has given researchers some interesting insights into SAD. A recent study of eighteen patients with social anxiety disorder and six controls without the disorder watched their cerebral blood flow as they performed "public" speaking to an audience of eight people, and "private" speaking without the audience. In the socially anxious patients, public speaking caused increased activity in the amygdala and decreased activity in the insular cortex and the right temporal pole, phenomena not seen in the control subjects. This kind of brain activity is consistent with that seen in a strong fear response as well.

Even the anticipation of public speaking can cause changes in cerebral blood flow. Another PET scan study divided a group of eighteen people with social anxiety into two groups, one assigned to speak alone before speaking to an audience of a half-dozen people, the other to do the reverse. Those who performed their private speech before their public one showed enhanced cerebral blood flow in the prefrontal cortex compared to the group who performed their public presentation prior to the private one.

It is known from numerous animal studies that the amygdala is largely responsible for processing emotions of fear and anxiety, and so brain research on social anxiety disorder has concentrated on this structure. One study looked at the effect of the amygdala on the perception of other human faces. It is known that newborn monkeys who have damage to the amygdala show increased fear near other monkeys. Similarly, people with damage to the amygdala are unable to make accurate social judgments of others based on facial expression—to determine, for example, what emotion a person is feeling by looking at his face. Using fMRI, the study showed that people with generalized social anxiety exhibited sharper amygdala responses to angry facial expressions versus happy facial expressions than did people who did not have social anxiety disorder. In other words, people with SAD demonstrate a kind of excessive reaction compared to other people, and although the researchers draw no firm conclusions, this suggests that a malfunctioning amygdala may play a role in producing the symptoms of social anxiety.

Studies with macaque monkeys, which have complex behaviors and social structures approximating those of humans, have also revealed some interesting facts about social life and the amygdala. Monkeys with experimentally induced lesions of the amygdala radically change their social behavior. In one study, monkeys with damaged amygdalas became much more interested and less fearful of new objects than normal monkeys. They also became much more social. Macaque monkeys are typically extremely shy with each other on first meeting, but monkeys with damaged amygdalas demonstrate no shyness at all. These monkeys skipped completely the usual tentative introductory phases of familiarization and began immediately to engage in social behaviors even with animals they had never met before. You would think that the normal monkeys would find this kind of behavior off-putting, but researchers were surprised to see that these amygdala-damaged monkeys were actually welcomed much more warmly by other monkeys than those without such damage. Their outgoing behavior actually engendered the same attitude in their normal companions!

These researchers worked with the hypothesis that the amygdala functions as a kind of social brake system, allowing the animal to assess fearful situations and react accordingly. This would happen not only in social interactions, but also in other instances of threat—assessing danger from a predator, for example. In humans, the physiological reactions provoked by the real danger of a physical threat are the same as those provoked by the falsely perceived danger of a benign social interaction, and it may well be that their place of origin in the brain is the same.

The amygdala is not the only brain structure involved in social behavior. For example, the prefrontal cortex works with the amygdala to modify responses to social situations, especially in modifying fear responses. FMRI studies have demonstrated that other parts of the brain are involved in panic disorder, phobias, and post-traumatic stress disorder.

Physiology and Shyness

Researchers have used various methods to try to isolate any physiological phenomena that could be directly connected to social anxiety disorder and no other cause. In addition to brain imaging, chemical challenge experiments, measuring hormonal levels, checking sleep patterns, and examining the heart rate and flushing symptoms characteristic of the disorder have all been looked at for clues.

Some ingenious studies with mice have identified a specific neuropeptide—oxytocin—as essential to remembering social interactions. A male mouse presented with a new member of its species will smell its head and ano-genital region for about one minute. When the same mouse is re-presented, the mouse will smell it only for a few seconds—it has registered a social memory of the mouse and doesn't need to go any further in its exploration to know who it is. But otherwise perfectly normal mice who have been genetically engineered to lack the gene that produces oxytocin can never remember who they've met and who they haven't. Even though all of their other mental processes are intact, any mouse, no matter how often they have met him, seems novel. If you inject such a mouse with oxytocin just before he meets a new mouse, he then remembers who he met, and recognizes him the next time he meets him. It doesn't help to inject him after his social encounter, only before. So oxytocin is actually essential to recording the memory of the social interaction, but not essential to recording other kinds of memory. Other experimenters have injected infusions of oxytocin into the brains of male rats, with the result that they become more socially interactive with other male rats. Clearly oxytocin is an important chemical in the social life of these animals, and, since oxytocin is present in all mammalian species including humans, there is good reason to believe that it is important in human social interactions as well.

Other animal experiments have added information about exactly where the oxytocin is working in the brain, and, not surprisingly, the amygdala turns out to be one important location. There are two species of small rodents called voles that live in North America. The species are genetically very closely related, but one, the montane vole, tends to be asocial, having interactions with other members of its species only when mating, while the other, the prairie vole, is very social, spending most of its time in physical contact with other prairie voles. Yet the levels of oxytocin in these two species are about the same. What is different is that the prairie vole has high levels of receptors for oxytocin in its amygdala, while the montane vole has high levels of such receptors in another part of the brain, the lateral septum. Injecting montane voles with oxytocin doesn't make them any more social—they're processing the oxytocin in the wrong part of the brain!

~

It is common now to hear people speak of mental illness as "a chemical imbalance in the brain," and this description, however vague and metaphoric, has a degree of accuracy to it. Dopamine is a neurotransmitter, a chemical released at the nerve endings in the brain to move electrical signals from one nerve to another. It has been implicated in

SAD. Researchers have observed that submissive behavior in primates is in some ways similar to the behavior of people with SAD. In subordinate female monkeys, it has been discovered, the transmission of dopamine is impaired. The chronic stress of being subordinate has led to physiological changes in brain function. Imaging studies in humans have revealed a similar malfunction in dopamine transmission in people suffering from social anxiety disorder.

Studies of neurotransmitters in social anxiety disease are in their infancy, and it is still impossible to draw definitive conclusions about their role in the disorder. Many other neurotransmitters function in the biology of anxiety disorders as well—corticotropin-releasing hormone, the monoaminergic transmitters, norepinephrine, serotonin, gamma-aminobutyric acid, and glutamate, among others, and sorting out what each of these do, and where in the brain they do it, is far from a finished task. Even some of the basics are still in question. For example, while it is well documented that serotonin reuptake inhibitors are effective in treating social phobia (see chapter 10), the precise action of serotonin in the disease is still for the most part a mystery. Dopamine-blocking agents have been shown to provoke social anxiety, and there are reports of successful treatment of social anxiety with dopamine agonists. There is at least one study demonstrating that people who have both panic disorder and social anxiety have decreased levels of one of dopamine's by-products in their cerebrospinal fluid. But again, exactly what dopamine does in the brain and how it affects disease is poorly understood.

Still, in light of these discoveries about the role of various chemicals in the biology and physiology of the brain, it becomes clearer that a "chemical imbalance in the brain" is probably at least part of the explanation for SAD. Humans with social anxiety disorder react to social situations with the same kinds of physiological activity produced by fear: increased heartbeat, sweating, heightened vigilance, and so on. In other words, people with SAD experience a fight or flight reaction to situations that, by any reasonable standard, don't require one. In animals, these are the symptoms produced when an animal is startled. And some researchers have even proposed that the startle reflex might be a useful tool in evaluating the extent of social anxiety in human patients.

One particular chemical receptor in the body that has drawn the attention of researchers on social anxiety is called the peripheral benzodiazepine receptor, or PBR. These receptors are located on cells throughout the body, and researchers now suspect that these PBRs play a role in social anxiety by regulating the production of the hormones that produce the symptoms of stress. In fact, the drugs used to treat anxiety have been found to alter the density of PBRs in the cells, thus reducing the symptoms of anxiety. Moreover, it is only in the anxiety disorders, including social anxiety, that abnormal density of PBRs is found—it doesn't happen with major depression, obsessive-compulsive disorder, or schizophrenia.

Shyness and Physical Health

The physiologic changes in the body associated with social anxiety disorder may affect other aspects of health as well. It has been well-known for hundreds of years that mood can affect physical health—the ancient Greek physician Galen observed that shy or melancholic people seemed more prone to infection than others, and the association of heart disease and depression is well established. A recent study at the University of California at Los Angeles School of Medicine has actually put some numbers on this phenomenon in an experiment involving a group of fifty-four men under treatment for early HIV infection—that is, men infected with the virus but as yet showing no symptoms of AIDS. They tested them for social inhibition, dividing them into more and less socially inhibited groups before beginning treatment with antiretroviral drugs. They found that socially inhibited men showed eight times poorer suppression of plasma viremia after three to twelve months of antiretroviral treatment when compared to the remainder of the sample group. They point out that the release of norepinephrine, a response in social anxiety, may accelerate virus replication, and they hypothesize that that is what was happening with their subjects. Treatment of social anxiety, this research suggests, may be a possible target for adjunctive therapy in the treatment of incompletely suppressed HIV infection.

Chemicals can be used to distinguish one psychiatric illness from another. Panic disorder, for example, has symptoms very much like those of social anxiety disorder, but scientists have shown that the symptoms of each disease are caused by different chemicals. A "challenge study" uses a drug or compound to mimic the symptoms of anxiety that occurs naturally. People suffering from panic disorder when challenged with an injection of sodium lactate, for example, develop all the symptoms of a panic attack—increased heartbeat, sweating, tremor, and so on. But if you give sodium lactate to people suffering from anxiety disorder, they have a reaction no greater than normal controls. The symptoms of the two disorders may look the same, in other words, but the chemical processes, the parts of the brain, and the kinds of receptors that are producing them are different. Of course, it's never so simple. A large dose of caffeine will produce the same anxiety reaction in people with panic disorder as it produces in those with social anxiety disorder. Like much of the research in neurobiology, the studies are not definitive, and are still subject to interpretation. But each of these research areas helps in beginning to define a biology of social anxiety disorder.

❧

Okay—I treat people, not monkeys, mice, or prairie voles, and it's a long way from suggestions and hypotheses like these to any useful clinical application of such knowledge. But researchers are now gradually beginning to figure out the neurobiology of behavior, and understanding this will undoubtedly prove immensely helpful in developing effective medicines to treat psychiatric illnesses. If, as we now suspect, a malfunctioning amygdala or a complex group of chemically mediated neurological processes is at the root of social anxiety disorder, and we can deepen our understanding of the biological processes at work, then it becomes possible to develop targeted medicines to correct biological malfunctions. For patients, this is the ultimate promise of this complex and difficult research.

Resources

National Organizations

Except for the National Institute of Mental Health, which is a governmental body, these organizations are primarily interested in advocacy on behalf of the mentally ill and their families. They also provide support in the form of reliable publications, useful websites, and referral services.

The Anxiety Disorders Association of America (ADAA)
8730 Georgia Avenue, Suite 600
Silver Spring, MD 20910
Tel: 240-485-1001; Fax: 240-485-1035
http://www.adaa.org/
Provides referrals to therapists, support groups, advises on insurance reimbursement and other advocacy issues.

The International Paruresis Association
P.O. Box 65111
Baltimore, MD 21209
Tel: 800-247-3864
http://www.paruresis.org/

National Alliance for the Mentally Ill (NAMI)
Colonial Place Three
2107 Wilson Blvd., Suite 300

Arlington, VA 22201-3042
Tel: 703-524-7600; Fax: 703-524-9094
HelpLine: 800-950-NAMI (6264)
http://www.nami.org
The largest advocacy group for the mentally ill.

National Association of Cognitive-Behavioral Therapists
P.O. Box 2195
Weirton, WV 26062
Tel: 800-853-1135; Outside U.S.: 304-723-3982; Fax: 304-723-3982
An educational and credentialing organization for cognitive behavioral therapists.

National Institute of Mental Health
5600 Fishers Lane, Room 7CO2
Bethesda, MD 20892-8030
Facts on Demand: 301-443-5158
http://www.nimh.nih.gov

National Mental Health Association (NMHA)
2001 N. Beauregard Street, 12th Floor
Alexandria, VA 22311
Tel: 703-684-7722; Fax: 703-684-5968
http://www.nmha.org

Selective Mutism Foundation
P.O. Box 13133
Sissonville, WV 25360-0133
http://www.selectivemutismfoundation.org

Hospital Anxiety Centers

Hospital clinics may be more carefully regulated and easier to research than private institutions, but variations in quality and expertise among these centers may complicate treatment, since your case may be suitable to a particular research protocol. The following is by no means a comprehensive listing.

Adult Anxiety Clinic of Temple University
Department of Psychology
Temple University, 419 Weiss Hall
1701 N. 13th Street
Philadelphia, PA 19122
E-mail: phobia@temple.edu

American Institute for Cognitive Therapy
136 East 57th Street, Suite 1101
New York, NY 10022
Tel: 212-308-2440

Anxiety and Traumatic Stress Disorders Research Program
University of California at San Diego
Tel: 858-622-6108
E-mail: veryshy@ucsd.edu

Duke Child and Family Study Center
718 Rutherford Road
Durham, NC 27705
Tel: 919-419-3474

Johns Hopkins University School of Medicine
Department of Psychiatry and Behavioral Sciences
600 North Wolfe Street
Baltimore, MD 21287-7131
Tel: 410-955-6111

Mount Sinai School of Medicine
Department of Psychiatry
One Gustave L. Levy Place, Box 1230
New York, NY 10029
Tel: 212-659-8716; Fax: 212-987-4031
E-mail: compulsion@mssm.edu

New York State Psychiatric Institute Anxiety Disorders Clinic
1051 Riverside Drive
New York, NY 10032
Tel: 212-543-5367
http://www.nyspi.org/Kolb/index.htm

Yale Department of Psychiatry Anxiety Disorders Research Clinic
100 York Street, #2J
New Haven, CT 06511
Tel: 203-764-9939

Websites and Newsgroups

Cognitive therapy, as well as other kinds of therapy for social anxiety, is practiced by many different kinds of professionals with many different levels of training. Anyone can open a website or contribute to a newsgroup on the Internet. We list these sites for information only, with no recommendations or guarantees. Some are the websites of individual practitioners who represent themselves as "Institutes," "Societies," or "Associations." Such nomenclature has no special meaning in law or medicine. Some are chat sites where one can connect with other people who suffer from social anxiety. This can certainly be useful to some people, but it is usually not a substitute for professional care. Websites listed were accessed in the spring of 2004.

alt.support.shyness; news:alt.support.shyness
Shyness newsgroup

alt.support.social-phobia; news:alt.support.social-phobia
Social phobia newsgroup

Anxiety and Phobia Peer Support Network
http://www.anxietytofreedom.com/

Anxiety Network
http://www.anxietynetwork.com
A large website with many links to information on all types of anxiety, provides information on the three common anxiety disorders: social anxiety, panic disorder, and generalized anxiety.

In the SpotLight
http://www.performanceanxiety.com/
About stage fear. Stories, workshops to sign up for, books to order, links to more information.

Selective Mutism Group, Child Anxiety Disorders Network, Inc.
http://www.selectivemutism.org/

Shyness.com
http://www.shyness.com/
An index to resources for shyness, includes upcoming events and surveys.

Social Anxiety/Facts for Health
http://socialanxiety.factsforhealth.org/
General information and pointers.

Social Anxiety Help
http://www.socialanxietyhelp.com/
Lots of information about cognitive behavioral therapy (CBT) for social anxiety disorder.

Social Anxiety Network
http://www.social-anxiety-network.com/
General information articles, CBT info, links, stuff to order.

Social Anxiety Support (SAS)
http://socialanxietysupport.com/index.htm
Discussion forums and chat services devoted to social anxiety.

Social Anxiety Australia
http://www.socialanxiety.com.au/
Comprehensive Australian website devoted to SAD.

Social Phobia/Social Anxiety Association
Thomas A. Richards, Ph.D., President
2058 E. Topeka Drive
Phoenix, AZ 85024
http://www.socialphobia.org/

Social Phobia Statements
http://members.tripod.com/~SocialPhobia/SocialPhobia1.html
"These are statements that helped me make progress against my social phobia. . . ."

Socialfear.com
http://www.socialfear.com/
Briefly and clearly reviews effective and recent SAD treatment medical approaches. Suggestions rely on personal experience and scientific publications.

www.social-anxiety.org
An educational resource supported by a grant from GlaxoSmithKline Pharmaceuticals.

Books on Social Anxiety for Non-Professionals

Beck, A. *Anxiety Disorders and Phobias: A Cognitive Perspective.* New York: Basic Books, 1985.

Berent, Jonathan, and Amy Lemley. *Beyond Shyness.* New York: Simon & Schuster, 1993.

Markway, Barbara G., and Gregory P. Markway. *Painfully Shy: How to Overcome Social Anxiety and Reclaim Your Life.* New York: St. Martin's Press, 2001.

Markway, Barbara G., Cheryl N. Carmin, C. Alec Pollard, and Teresa Flynn. *Dying of Embarrassment: Help for Social Anxiety & Phobia.* Oakland, Calif.: New Harbinger Publications, 1992.

Rapee, Ronald M. *Overcoming Shyness and Social Phobia: A Step-by-Step Guide.* Northvale, N.J.: Jason Aronson, Inc., 1998.

Schneier, Franklin, and Lawrence Welkowitz. *The Hidden Face of Shyness: Understanding and Overcoming Social Anxiety.* New York: Avon, 1996.

Stein, Murray B., and John R. Walker. *Triumph Over Shyness.* New York: McGraw Hill, 2002.

Stein, Murray B., ed. *Social Phobia: Clinical and Research Perspectives.* Washington, D.C.: American Psychiatric Press, 1995.

Scientific Bibliography

This selection of scientific articles on the subject of social anxiety disorder was used in preparing this book. For the most part, these are quite technical, written by professionals and directed at other professionals. But reading any of them will give you an idea about the kinds of research going on and the interesting discoveries being made in this area. In addition, such reading will show you how psychiatric research is carried out and how the scientific method is applied in thinking about mental disorders.

Journal Abbreviations

Acta Psychiatr Scand: Acta Psychiatrica Scandinavia
Am J Psychiatry: American Journal of Psychiatry
Arch Gen Psychiatry: Archives of General Psychiatry
Behav Res Ther: Behaviour Research and Therapy
Biol Psychiatry: Biological Psychiatry
Br J Psychiatry: British Journal of Psychiatry
Clin Psych Rev: Clinical Psychology Review
Depress Anxiety: Depression and Anxiety
Dev Psych: Developmental Psychology
Eur Arch Psychiatry Clin Neurosci: European Archives of Psychiatry and Clinical Neuroscience
Eur Psychiatry: European Psychiatry: The Journal of the Association of European Psychiatrists

Int J Eat Disord: International Journal of Eating Disorders
Int J Neuropsychopharmacol: International Journal of Neuropsychopharmacology
J Abnorm Child Psychol: Journal of Abnormal Child Psychology
J Affect Disord: Journal of Affective Disorders
J Am Acad Child Adolesc Psychiatry: Journal of the American Academy of Child and Adolescent Psychiatry
J Anxiety Disord: Journal of Anxiety Disorders
J Child Psychol Psychiatry: Journal of Child Psychology and Psychiatry
J Clin Psychiatry: Journal of Clinical Psychiatry
J Clin Psychol: Journal of Clinical Psychology
J Clin Psychopharmacol: Journal of Clinical Psychopharmacology
J Consult Clin Psychol: Journal of Consulting and Clinical Psychology
J Educ Psychol: Journal of Educational Psychology
J Exp Psychol Anim Behav Process: Journal of Experimental Psychology. Animal Behavior Processes
J Nerv Ment Dis: Journal of Nervous and Mental Disorders
J Sch Health: Journal of School Health
JAMA: Journal of the American Medical Association
Pharmacol Biochem Behav: Pharmacology, Biochemistry, and Behavior
Psychiatry Res: Psychiatric Research
Psychol Assess: Psychological Assessment
Psychol Med: Psychological Medicine
Psychother Psychosom: Psychotherapy and Psychosomatics
Trends Cogn Sci: Trends in Cognitive Sciences

Introduction: A "New" Disease?

Katzelnick, D. J., K. A. Kobak, T. DeLeire, et al. "Impact of generalized social anxiety disorder in managed care." *Am J Psychiatry* 158(12) (December 2001): 1999–2007.

Chapter 1: Who Gets Social Anxiety, and Why?

Beidel, D. C., S. M. Turner, T. L. Morris. "Psychopathology of childhood social phobia." *J Am Acad Child Adolesc Psychiatry* 38(6) (June 1999): 643–50.
Biederman, J., D. R. Hirshfeld-Becker, J. F. Rosenbaum, et al. "Further evidence of association between behavioral inhibition and social anxiety in children." *Am J Psychiatry* 158(10) (October 2001): 1673–79.
Biederman, J., J. F. Rosenbaum, E. A. Bolduc, et al. "A high-risk study of young children of parents with panic disorder and agoraphobia with and without comorbid major depression." *Psychiatry Res* 37(3) (June 1991): 333–48.
Caspi, A., G. H. Elder, D. J. Bem. "Moving away from the world: life-course patterns of shy children." *Dev Psych* 24 (1988): 824–31.

Chartier, M. J., J. R. Walker, M. B. Stein. "Social phobia and potential childhood risk factors in a community sample." *Psychol Med* 31(2) (February 2001): 307–15.

Clarvit, S. R., F. R. Schneier, M. R. Liebowitz. "The offensive subtype of Taijin-kyofu-sho in New York City: the phenomenology and treatment of a social anxiety disorder." *J Clin Psychiatry* 57(11) (November 1996): 523–27.

Cook, M., S. Mineka. Selective associations in the observational conditioning of fear in rhesus monkeys. *J Exp Psychol Anim Behav Process* 16(4) (October 1990): 372–89.

Cooper, P. J., M. Eke. "Childhood shyness and maternal social phobia: a community study." *Br J Psychiatry* 174 (May 1999): 439–43.

Darwin, Charles. *The Expression of the Emotions in Man and Animals* (New York: D. Appleton and Company, 1898), p. 311.

Degonda, M., J. Angst. "The Zurich study: 20. Social phobia and agoraphobia." *Eur Arch Psychiatry Clin Neurosci* 243(2) (1993): 95–102.

Fyer, A. J., S. Mannuzza, T. F. Chapman, et al. "A direct interview family study of social phobia." *Arch Gen Psychiatry* 50(4) (April 1993): 286–93.

Ge, X., K. M. Best, R. D. Conger, R. L. Simons. "Parenting behaviors and the occurrence and co-occurrence of adolescent depressive symptoms and conduct problems." *Dev Psych* 32(4) (July 1996): 717–31.

Ge, X., R. D. Conger, R. J. Cadoret, et al. "The developmental interface between nature and nurture: a mutual influence model of child antisocial behavior and parent behaviors." *Dev Psych* 32(4) (July 1996): 574–89.

Goldstein, R. B., P. J. Wickramaratne, E. Horwath, et al. "Familial aggregation and phenomenology of 'early'-onset (at or before age 20 years) panic disorder." *Arch Gen Psychiatry* 54(3) (March 1997): 271–78.

James, William. *Principles of Psychology,* vol. 2, chap. 24 (1890).

Kendler, K. S., J. Myers, C. A. Prescott. "Parenting and adult mood, anxiety and substance use disorders in female twins: an epidemiological, multi-informant, retrospective study." *Psychol Med* 30(2) (March 2000): 281–94.

Kendler, K. S., M. C. Neale, R. C. Kessler, et al. "The genetic epidemiology of phobias in women: the interrelationship of agoraphobia, social phobia, situational phobia, and simple phobia." *Arch Gen Psychiatry* 49(4) (April 1992): 273–81.

Kessler, R. C., M. B. Stein, P. Berglund. "Social phobia subtypes in the National Comorbidity Survey." *Am J Psychiatry* 155(5) (May 1998): 613–19.

Lieb, R., H. U. Wittchen, M. Hofler, et al. "Parental psychopathology, parenting styles, and the risk of social phobia in offspring: a prospective-longitudinal community study." *Arch Gen Psychiatry* 57(9) (September 2000): 859–66.

Magee, W. J., W. W. Eaton, H. U. Wittchen, et al. "Agoraphobia, simple phobia, and social phobia in the National Comorbidity Survey." *Arch Gen Psychiatry* 53(2) (February 1996): 159–68.

Mannuzza, S., F. R. Schneier, T. F. Chapman, et al. "Generalized social phobia: reliability and validity." *Arch Gen Psychiatry* 52(3) (March 1995): 230–37.

Matsunaga, H., N. Kiriike, T. Matsui, et al. "Taijin kyofusho: a form of social anxiety disorder that responds to serotonin reuptake inhibitors?" *Int J Neuropsychopharmacol* 4(3) (September 2001): 231–37.

Merikangas, K. R., S. Avenevoli, L. Dierker, et al. "Vulnerability factors among children at risk for anxiety disorders." *Biol Psychiatry* 46(11) (December 1999): 1523–35.

Merikangas, K. R., R. Lieb, H. U. Wittchen, et al. "Family and high-risk studies of social anxiety disorder." *Acta Psychiatr Scand* 108 Suppl 417 (September 2003): 28–37.

Ohman, A. "Face the beast and fear the face: animal and social fears as prototypes for evolutionary analyses of emotion." *Psychophysiology* 23(2) (March 1986): 123–45.

Rosenblum, L. A., J. D. Coplan, S. Friedman, et al. "Adverse early experiences affect noradrenergic and serotonergic functioning in adult primates." *Biol Psychiatry* 35(4) (February 1994): 221–27.

Safren, S. A., B. S. Gershuny, P. Marzol, et al. "History of childhood abuse in panic disorder, social phobia, and generalized anxiety disorder." *J Nerv Ment Dis* 190(7) (July 2002): 453–56.

Schneier, F. R., J. Johnson, C. D. Hornig, et al. "Social phobia: comorbidity and morbidity in an epidemiologic sample." *Arch Gen Psychiatry* 49(4) (April 1992): 282–88.

Skre, I., S. Onstad, S. Torgersen, et al. "A twin study of DSM-III-R anxiety disorders." *Acta Psychiatr Scand* 88(2) (August 1993): 85–92.

Spence, S. H., C. Donovan, M. Brechman-Toussaint. "The treatment of childhood social phobia: the effectiveness of a social skills training-based, cognitive-behavioral intervention, with and without parental involvement." *J Child Psychol Psychiatry* 41(6) (September 2000): 713–26.

Stein, M. B., M. J. Chartier, A. L. Hazen, et al. "A direct-interview family study of generalized social phobia." *Am J Psychiatry* 155(1) (January 1998): 90–97.

Townsley, R. "Social phobia: identification of possible etiological factors." Ph.D. diss., University of Georgia, Athens, Ga., 1992.

Turk, C. L., R. G. Heimberg, S. M. Orsillo, et al. "An investigation of gender differences in social phobia." *J Anxiety Disord* 12(3) (May–June 1998): 209–23.

Wittchen, H. U., C. B. Nelson, G. Lachner. "Prevalence of mental disorders and psychosocial impairments in adolescents and young adults." *Psychol Med* 28(1) (January 1998): 109–26.

Wittchen, H. U., M. B. Stein, R. C. Kessler. "Social fears and social phobia in a community sample of adolescents and young adults: prevalence, risk factors and comorbidity." *Psychol Med* 29(2) (March 1999): 309–23.

Chapter 2: Shyness, Phobia, Social Anxiety

Chavira, D. A., M. B. Stein, V. L. Malcarne. "Scrutinizing the relationship between shyness and social phobia." *J Anxiety Disord* 16(6) (2002): 585–98.

Fyer, A. J., S. Mannuzza, T. F. Chapman, et al. "A direct interview family study of social phobia." *Arch Gen Psychiatry* 50(4) (April 1993): 286–93.

Heiser, N. A., S. M. Turner, D. C. Beidel. "Shyness: relationship to social phobia and other psychiatric disorders." *Behav Res Ther* 41(2) (February 2003): 209–21.

Morris, L. W., M. A. Davis, C. H. Hutchings. "Cognitive and emotional components of anxiety: literature review and a revised worry-emotionality scale." *J Educ Psychol* 73(4) (August 1981): 541–55.

Chapter 3: Symptoms

Mennin, D. S., D. M. Fresco, R. G. Heimbert, et al. "Screening for social anxiety disorder in the clinical setting using the Liebowitz Social Anxiety Scale." *J Anxiety Disord* 16(6) (2002): 661–73.

Stein, M. B., C. A. Shea, T. W. Uhde. "Social phobic symptoms in patients with panic disorder: practical and theoretical implications." *Am J Psychiatry* 146(2) (February 1989): 235–38. Also, Van Ameringen, M., C. Mancini, G. Styan, et al. "Relationship of social phobia with other psychiatric illness." *J Affect Disord* 21(2) (February 1991): 93–99.

Stopa, L., D. M. Clark. "Cognitive processes in social phobia." *Behav Res Ther* 31(3) (March 1993): 255–67.

Chapter 4: More Than One Illness

Cole, S. W., M. E. Kemeny, J. L. Fahey, et al. "Psychological risk factors for HIV pathogenesis: mediation by the autonomic nervous system." *Biol Psychiatry* 54(12) (December 15, 2003): 1444–56.

Dierker, L. C., A. M. Albano, G. N. Clarke, et al. "Screening for anxiety and depression in early adolescence." *J Am Acad Child Adolesc Psychiatry* 40(8) (August 2001): 929–36.

Godart, N. T., M. F. Flament, Y. Lecrubier, et al. "Anxiety disorders in anorexia nervosa and bulimia nervosa: comorbidity and chronology of appearance." *Eur Psychiatry* 15(1) (February 2000): 38–45.

Goodwin, R. D., M. L. Fitzgibbon. "Social anxiety as a barrier to treatment for eating disorders." *Int J Eat Disord* 32(1) (July 2002): 103–6.

Hayward, C., S. Varady, A. M. Albano, et al. "Cognitive-behavioral group therapy for social phobia in female adolescents: results of a pilot study." *J Am Acad Child Adolesc Psychiatry* 39(6) (June 2000): 721–26.

Keller, M. B. "The lifelong course of social anxiety disorder: a clinical perspective." *Acta Psychiatr Scand* Suppl 417 (September 2003): 85–94.

Lepine, J. P., A. Pelissolo. "Social phobia and alcoholism: a complex relationship." *J Affect Disord* 50 Suppl 1 (September 1998): S23–28.

Merikangas, K. R., J. Angst. "Comorbidity and social phobia: evidence from clinical, epidemiologic, and genetic studies." *Eur Arch Psychiatry Clin Neurosci* 244(6) (1995): 297–303.

Nelson, E. C., J. D. Grant, K. K. Bucholz, et al. "Social phobia in a population-based female adolescent twin sample: comorbidity and associated suicide-related symptoms." *Psychol Med* 30(4) (July 2000): 797–804.

Parker, G., K. Wilhelm, P. Mitchell, et al. "The influence of anxiety as a risk to early onset major depression." *J Affect Disord* 52(1–3) (January–March 1999): 11–17.

Schneier, F. R., J. Johnson, C. D. Hornig, et al. "Social phobia: comorbidity and morbidity in an epidemiologic sample." *Arch Gen Psychiatry* 49(4) (April 1992): 282–88.

Wittchen, H. U., M. B. Stein, R. C. Kessler. "Social fears and social phobia in a community sample of adolescents and young adults: prevalence, risk factors and comorbidity." *Psychol Med* 29(2) (March 1999): 309–23.

Chapter 5: Are You Sure It's Social Anxiety?

Haxby, J. V., E. A. Hoffman, M. I. Gobbini. "The distributed human neural system for face perception." *Trends Cogn Sci* 4(6) (June 2000): 223–33.

Mattia, J. I., R. G. Heimberg, D. A. Hope. "The revised Stroop color-naming task in social phobics." *Behav Res Ther* 31(3) (March 1993): 305–13.

Rapee, R. M., R. G. Heimberg. "A cognitive-behavioral model of anxiety in social phobia." *Behav Res Ther* 35(8) (August 1997): 741–56.

Chapter 6: Children and Adolescents

Albano, A. M., B. F. Chorpita, P. M. Di Batolo, et al. "Comorbidity in a clinical sample of children and adolescents with anxiety disorders: characteristics and developmental considerations," unpublished ms., State University of New York at Albany, cited in Albano, A. M., "Social phobia in children and adolescents: current treatment approaches," paper presented at 5th Internet World Congress in Biomedical Sciences at McMaster University, Hamilton, Ontario, Canada, Dec. 1–16, 1998. Available at http://www.mcmaster.ca/inabis98/ameringen/albano0303/index.html.

Beidel, D. C., S. M. Turner, T. L. Morris. "Psychopathology of childhood social phobia." *J Am Acad Child Adolesc Psychiatry* 38(6) (June 1999): 643–50.

Black, B., T. W. Uhde. "Psychiatric characteristics of children with selective mutism: a pilot study." *J Am Acad Child Adolesc Psychiatry* 34(7) (July 1995): 847–56.

Ginsburg, G. S., A. M. La Greca, W. K. Silverman. "Social anxiety in children with anxiety disorders: relation with social and emotional functioning." *J Abnorm Child Psychol* 26(3) (June 1998): 175–85.

Kagan, J., J. S. Reznick, N. Snidman. "Biological bases of childhood shyness." *Science* 240(4849) (April 8, 1988): 167–71.

Lieb, R., H. U. Wittchen, M. Hofler, et al. "Parental psychopathology, parenting styles, and the risk of social phobia in offspring: a prospective-longitudinal community study." *Arch Gen Psychiatry* 57(9) (September 2000): 859–66.

Page, R. M. "Shyness as a risk factor for adolescent substance use." *J Sch Health* 59(10) (December 1989): 432–35.

Plomin, T., D. Daniels. "Genetics and Shyness," in W. H. Jones, J. M. Cheek, S. R. Briggs, eds. *Shyness: Perspectives on Research and Treatment* (New York: Plenum Press, 1986), pp. 63–80.

Prior, M., D. Smart, A. Sanson, et al. "Does shy-inhibited temperament in childhood lead to anxiety problems in adolescence?" *J Am Acad Child Adolesc Psychiatry* 39(4) (April 2000): 461–68.

Rosenbaum, J. F., J. Biederman, D. R. Hirshfeld, et al. "Further evidence of an association between behavioral inhibition and anxiety disorders: results from a family study of children from a non-clinical sample." *J Psychiatr Res* 25(1–2) (1991): 49–65.

Schwartz, C. E., N. Snidman, J. Kagan. "Adolescent social anxiety as an outcome of inhibited temperament in childhood." *J Am Acad Child Adolesc Psychiatry* 38(8) (August 1999): 1008–15.

Chapter 7: On Your Own: Self-Tests for Shyness and Exercises to Help Overcome It

Beidel, D. C., S. M. Turner, C. M. Fink. "Assessment of childhood social phobia: construct, convergent, and discriminative validity of the Social Phobia and Anxiety Inventory for Children (SPAI-C)." *Psychol Assess* 8 (1996): 235–40.

Beidel, D. C., S. M. Turner, T. L. Morris. "A new inventory to assess childhood social anxiety and phobia: the Social Phobia and Anxiety Inventory for Children." *Psychol Assess* 7(1) (March 1995): 73–79.

Connor, K. M., J. R. Davidson, L. E. Churchill, et al. "Psychometric properties of the Social Phobia Inventory (SPIN): new self-rating scale." *Br J Psychiatry* 176 (April 2000): 379–86.

Connor, K. M., K. A. Kobak, L. E. Churchill, et al. "Mini-SPIN: a brief screening assessment for generalized social anxiety disorder." *Depress Anxiety* 14(2) (2001): 137–40.

Davidson, J. R., C. M. Miner, J. De Veaugh-Geiss, et al. "The Brief Social Phobia Scale: a psychometric evaluation." *Psychol Med* 27(1) (January 1997): 161–66.

Dummit, E. S., R. G. Klein, N. K. Tancer, et al. "Systematic assessment of 50 children with selective mutism." *J Am Acad Child Adolesc Psychiatry* 36(5) May 1997: 653–60.

Liebowitz, M. R. "Social Phobia." *Modern Problems in Psychopharmacology* 22 (1987): 141–73.

Turner, S. M., M. R. Johnson, D. C. Beidel, et al. "The Social Thoughts and Beliefs Scale: a new inventory for assessing cognitions in social phobia." *Psychol Assess* 15(3) (September 2003): 384–91.

Chapter 8: Finding the Best Treatment

Wittchen, H. U., M. B. Stein, R. C. Kessler. "Social fears and social phobia in a community sample of adolescents and young adults: prevalence, risk factors and comorbidity." *Psychol Med* 29(2) (March 1999): 309–23.

Chapter 9: Psychological Treatments for Social Anxiety

Butler, G., A. Cullington, M. Munby, et al. "Exposure and anxiety management in the treatment of social phobia." *J Consult Clin Psychol* 52(4) (August 1984): 642–50.

Fava, G. A., S. Grandi, R. Canestrari. "Treatment of social phobia by homework exposure." *Psychother Psychosom* 52(4) (1989): 209–13.

Haemmerlie, F. M., R. L. Montgomery, J. Melchers. "Social support, perceptions of attractiveness, weight, and the CPI in socially anxious males and females." *J Clin Psychol* 44(3) (May 1988): 435–41.

Hope, D. A., R. G. Heimberg. "Public and private self-consciousness and social phobia." *J Pers Assess* 52(4) (Winter 1988): 626–39.

Juster, H. R., R. G. Heimberg. "Longitudinal course and long-term outcome of cognitive-behavioral treatment." *Psychiatr Clin North Am* 18(4) (December 1995): 821–42.

Lipsitz, J. D., R. D. Marshall. "Alternative psychotherapy approaches for social anxiety disorder." *Psychiatr Clin North Am* 24(4) (December 2001): 817–29.

Rapee, R. M., R. G. Heimberg. "A cognitive-behavioral model of anxiety in social phobia." *Behav Res Ther* 35(8) (August 1997): 741–56.

Somer, E. "Biofeedback-aided hypnotherapy for intractable phobic anxiety." *Am J Clin Hypn* 37(3) (January 1995): 54–64.

Stopa, L., D. M. Clark. "Cognitive processes in social phobia." 31(3) *Behav Res Ther* (March 1993): 255–67.

Turner, S. M., D. C. Beidel, R. G. Jacob. "Social phobia: a comparison of behavior therapy and atenolol." *J Consult Clin Psychol* 62(2) (April 1994): 350–58.

Chapter 10: Pharmacological Treatments for Social Anxiety

Emmanuel, N. P., O. Brawman-Mintzer, W. A. Morton, et al. "Bupropion-SR in treatment of social phobia." *Depress Anxiety* 12(2) (2000): 111–13.

Gelernter, C. S., T. W. Uhde, P. Cimbolic, et al. "Cognitive-behavioral and pharmacological treatments of social phobia: a controlled study." *Arch Gen Psychiatry* 48(10) (October 1991): 938–45.

Heimberg, R. G., M. R. Liebowitz, D. A. Hope, et al. "Cognitive behavioral group therapy vs. phenelzine therapy for social phobia: 12-week outcome." *Arch Gen Psychiatry* 55(12) (December 1998): 1133–41.

Kobak, K. A., J. H. Greist, J. W. Jefferson, et al. "Fluoxetine in social phobia: a double-blind, placebo-controlled pilot study." *J Clin Psychopharmacol* 22(3) (June 2002): 257–62.

Pande, A. C., J. R. Davidson, J. W. Jefferson, et al. "Treatment of social phobia with gabapentin: a placebo-controlled study." *J Clin Psychopharmacol* 19(4) (August 1999): 341–48.

Research Units on Pediatric Psychopharmacology Anxiety Study Group: Walkup, J., M. Labellarte, M. A. Riddle, et al. "Treatment of pediatric anxiety disorders: an open-label extension of the research units on pediatric psychophar-macology anxiety study." *J Child Adolesc Psychopharmacol* 12(3) (Fall 2002): 175–88.

Simpson, H. B., F. R. Schneier, R. B. Campeas, et al. "Imipramine in the treatment of social phobia." *J Clin Psychopharmacol* 18(2) (April 1998): 132–35.

Stein, M. B., M. R. Liebowitz, R. B. Lydiard, et al. "Paroxetine treatment of generalized social phobia (social anxiety disorder): a randomized controlled trial." *JAMA* 280(8) (August 26, 1998): 708–13.

Turner, S. M., D. C. Beidel, R. G. Jacob. "Social phobia: a comparison of behavior therapy and atenolol." *J Consult Clin Psychol* 62(2) (April 1994): 350–58.

Van Ameringen, M. A., R. M. Lane, J. R. Walker, et al. "Sertraline treatment of generalized social phobia: a 20-week, double-blind, placebo-controlled study." *Am J Psychiatry* 158(2) (February 2001): 275–81.

Walker, J. R., M. A. Van Ameringen, R. Swinson, et al. "Prevention of relapse in generalized social phobia: results of a 24-week study in responders to 20 weeks of sertraline treatment." *J Clin Psychopharmacol* 20(6) (December 2000): 636–44.

Chapter 11: Making Your Own Contribution to Clinical Research

Baker, C. B., M. T. Johnsrud, M. L. Crismon, et al. "Quantitative analysis of sponsorship bias in economic studies of antidepressants." *Br J Psychiatry* 183(6) (December 2003): 498–506.

Lexchin, J., L. A. Bero, B. Djulbegovic, et al. "Pharmaceutical industry spon-sorship and research outcome and quality: systematic review." *BMJ* 326(7400) (May 31, 2003): 1167–70.

Conclusion: Social Anxiety and the Brain—New Research

Amaral, D. G. "The primate amygdala and the neurobiology of social behav-ior: implications for understanding social anxiety." *Biol Psychiatry* 51(1) (January 2002): 11–17.

Cole, S. W., M. E. Kemeny, J. L. Fahey, et al. "Psychological risk factors for HIV pathogenesis: mediation by the autonomic nervous system." *Biol Psychiatry* 54(12) (December 15, 2003): 1444–56.

Drugan, R. C., A. S. Basile, J. N. Crawley, et al. "Characterization of stress-induced alterations in [3H] Ro5-4864 binding to peripheral benzodiazepine receptors in rat heart and kidney." *Pharmacol Biochem Behav* 30(4) (August 1988): 1015–20.

Grillon, C., W. A. Falls, R. Ameli, et al. "Safety signals and human anxiety: a fear-potentiated startle study." *Anxiety* 1(1) (1994): 13–21.

Kasper, S. "Social phobia: the nature of the disorder." *J Affect Disord* 50 Suppl 1 (September 1998): S3–9.

Schwartz, C. E., C. I. Wright, L. M. Shin, et al. "Inhibited and uninhibited infants "grown up": adult amygdalar response to novelty." *Science* 300(5627) (June 20, 2003): 1952–53.

Stein, M. B., P. R. Goldin, J. Sareen, et al. "Increased amygdala activation to angry and contemptuous faces in generalized social phobia." *Arch Gen Psychiatry* 59(11) (November 2002): 1027–34.

Tillfors M., T. Furmark, I. Marteinsdottir, et al. "Cerebral blood flow in subjects with social phobia during stressful speaking tasks: a PET study." *Am J Psychiatry* 158(8) (August 2001): 1220–26.

Tillfors, M., T. Furmark, I. Marteinsdottir, et al. "Cerebral blood flow during anticipation of public speaking in social phobia: a PET study." *Biol Psychiatry* 52(11) (December 2002): 1113–19.

Acknowledgments

I first would like to acknowledge the wonderful collaborative relationship I have had with Nick Bakalar, a skilled writer of good humor and great insight. I also acknowledge my very productive, long-standing collaborations with Dan Stein, M.D., who edited the *American Psychiatric Publishing Textbook of Anxiety Disorders* with me, Daphne Simeon, M.D., who edited *The Concise Guide to Anxiety Disorders* with me, and Marc Summers, who wrote *Everything in Its Place: My Trials and Triumphs with Obsessive-Compulsive Disorder* with me. I am indebted to Francine Cournos, M.D., who read the manuscript and made many useful suggestions for improvements.

I also thank the following colleagues: Stefano Pallanti, M.D., Joseph Zohar, M.D., Naomi Fineberg, M.D., Lorrin Koran, M.D., Katherine Phillips, M.D., Kenneth L. Davis, M.D., Jack Gorman, M.D., Larry Siever, M.D., Donald F. Klein, M.D., Michael Liebowitz, M.D., Daphne Simeon, M.D., Andrea Allen, Ph.D., Sallie Jo Hadley, M.D., Stacey Wasserman, M.D., Evdokia Anagnostou,

M.D., Latha Soorya, Ph.D., Ann Phillips, Ph.D., Bill Chaplin, Ph.D., Hirschell and DeAnna Levine and Jack Cohen of the Seaver Foundation, and Paula and Bill Oppenheim of the PBO Foundation.

Acknowledgment is also due for research grants from the National Institute of Mental Health, the National Institute of Neurological Disorders and Stroke, the National Institute of Drug Abuse, the Orphan Products Division of the Food and Drug Administration, as well as Solvay Pharmaceuticals, Wyeth Laboratories, Pfizer, Abbott, UCB Pharma, GlaxoSmithKline, and Lilly Research Laboratories. I acknowledge as well the important work that the Anxiety Disorders Association of America and its founder, Jerilyn Ross, M.A., L.I.C.S.W., does on behalf of anxiety disorder sufferers.

Finally both Nick Bakalar and I are thankful for the splendid editorial work of Lisa Considine, whose well-sharpened blue pencil has made the book much better than it would otherwise have been. We are also grateful for, and mightily impressed by, the sharp-eyed copyediting of Erin Clermont.

Index

About the Authors

ERIC HOLLANDER, M.D., is a professor of psychiatry at Mount Sinai Medical School in New York City. He is the coauthor of the American Psychiatric Association's *Textbook of Anxiety Disorders* and has appeared on *Dateline* and *The Today Show*.

NICHOLAS BAKALAR is the author or coauthor of eleven books, including *Understanding Teenage Depression*.